T0288289

THE BRIDGE STREET HISTORY CENTER
OF GRANBURY, TEXAS,

presents

Civil War

CAMPAIGNS
in the
WEST

STEVEN E. WOODWORTH
AND CHARLES D. GREAR
SERIES EDITORS

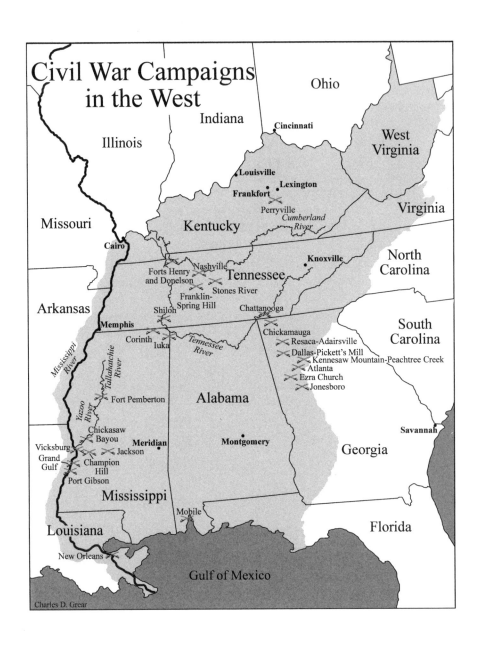

Civil War Campaigns
in the West

Ohio

Indiana

Cincinnati

Illinois

West
Virginia

Louisville
Lexington
Frankfort

Virginia

Perryville
Cumberland
River

Missouri

Kentucky

Cairo

North
Carolina

Knoxville

Nashville

Forts Henry
and Donelson

Tennessee

Stones River

Franklin-
Spring Hill

Shiloh

Chattanooga

Arkansas

Memphis

South
Carolina

Corinth
Iuka

Chickamauga

Resaca-Adairsville

Dallas-Pickett's Mill
Kennesaw Mountain-Peachtree Creek
Atlanta
Ezra Church
Jonesboro

Tennessee
River

Tallahatchie
River

Fort Pemberton

Alabama

Yazoo
River

Mississippi
River

Savannah

Chickasaw
Bayou

Meridian

Montgomery

Georgia

Vicksburg
Jackson

Grand
Gulf

Champion
Hill

Port Gibson

Mississippi

Mobile

Florida

Louisiana

New Orleans

Gulf of Mexico

Charles D. Grear

The

VICKSBURG

Assaults

MAY 19–22, 1863

Edited by Steven E. Woodworth
and Charles D. Grear

Southern Illinois University Press
Carbondale

Southern Illinois University Press
www.siupress.com

22 21 20 19   4 3 2 1

Jacket illustration: painting (cropped), *First at Vicksburg*, by
an unknown artist, part of the U.S. Army Center of Military
History's U.S. Army in Action series, depicting the Union's
First Battalion, 13th Infantry, attacking the Confederate lines
at Vicksburg, Mississippi, on May 19, 1863. Courtesy of the U.S.
Army Center of Military History and Wikimedia Commons.

Publication of this book has been financially supported by the
Bridge Street History Center of Granbury, Texas.

Library of Congress Cataloging-in-Publication Data
Names: Woodworth, Steven E., editor. | Grear, Charles D.,
[date] editor.
Title: The Vicksburg assaults, May 19-22, 1863 / edited by
Steven E. Woodworth and Charles D. Grear.
Description: Carbondale : Southern Illinois University Press,
[2019] | Series: Civil war campaigns in the West | Includes
bibliographical references and index.
Identifiers: LCCN 2018048726 | ISBN 9780809337194 (cloth :
alk. paper) | ISBN 9780809337200 (e-book)
Subjects: LCSH: Vicksburg (Miss.)—History—Siege, 1863. |
Mississippi—History—Civil War, 1861-1865—Campaigns. |
United States—History—Civil War, 1861-1865—Campaigns.
Classification: LCC E475.27 .V614 2019 | DDC 973.7/344—dc23
LC record available at https://lccn.loc.gov/2018048726

Printed on recycled paper. ♻

This paper meets the requirements of ANSI/NISO Z39.48-1992
(Permanence of Paper) ∞

To my patient and understanding wife, Edna Garza Grear

Again, for Leah

CONTENTS

ILLUSTRATIONS

Maps

Figures (following page 90)

ACKNOWLEDGMENTS

Anthologies by nature cannot be developed without the help of many people. We, the editors, serve only a small role in creating this volume. The staff of Southern Illinois University Press continues to dedicate countless hours throughout every step of the publishing process. Thank you. The contributors deserve our deepest gratitude. Their scholarship and dedication to their craft made it a pleasure to work on this book—most important, it could not exist without them. Thank you all. As always, the highest praise and distinct recognition goes to Southern Illinois University Press editor Sylvia Frank Rodrigue for all her efforts. Sylvia not only campaigns for our books and goes above and beyond what is expected of any editor but also keeps us on task and motivates us throughout the process. We cannot praise her hard work and expertise enough; thank you, Sylvia. Lastly, we would like to express our deepest appreciation to our families for their constant support. They inspire us in all our endeavors.

The Vicksburg Assaults

MAY 19–22, 1863

INTRODUCTION

Charles D. Grear

From March 29 to May 18, 1863, General Ulysses S. Grant's Army of the Tennessee campaigned in Mississippi, overwhelming all Confederate forces they encountered with the goal of capturing Vicksburg, the Confederate stronghold on the Mississippi River. Every Union victory improved morale and after the fight at Big Black River Bridge on May 17, Grant's forces continued to gain momentum. Now within miles of Vicksburg, Federal soldiers felt the end of the campaign was in sight. One more quick victory could end the campaign, with the Union gaining control of the Mississippi and dividing the Confederacy in half. Prospects such as these motivated officers and their men alike to assault the Confederate defenses consolidating around Vicksburg.

Conversely, on May 17, Confederate general John C. Pemberton ordered the demoralized Army of Mississippi to retreat to the defensive lines surrounding Vicksburg. Pemberton brought his main force west from the Big Black River Bridge, John H. Forney and Martin Luther Smith moved their divisions southward from the Yazoo bluffs, and John Moore's brigade retreated north from Warrenton to reinforce Vicksburg. As Confederate soldiers moved into trenches dug months before, fatigue and demoralization spread throughout the ranks. Sensing the dejection of his men, Pemberton announced that he planned to hold Vicksburg until the last. Though his proclamation was melodramatic, with rhetoric of fighting to the last and only then "selling" Vicksburg to the enemy, the men appreciated his guile and Confederate morale began to improve.

Immediately on May 18 Pemberton began to organize his defenses and strengthen Confederate positions. Soldiers quickly dug out the trenches partially filled by erosion and began connecting them to one another. During the day, Pemberton received orders from General Joseph E. Johnston to abandon the city and join his "Army of Relief." That night Pemberton summoned his generals to his headquarters for the infamous Council-of-War. At the council, he read aloud Johnston's orders to evacuate Vicksburg and then put their next move to a vote. Pemberton's generals all voted to defend this vital city to the Southern heartland, recognizing there was too much to lose if they abandoned Vicksburg. There were too many supplies stored in the city that the Confederacy could not afford to replace if they gave up control of the Mississippi River. If they had followed Johnston's orders, the Army of Mississippi would remain intact, but they would concede defeat to the Union, lose most of their supplies, and isolate the Trans-Mississippi from the rest of the Confederacy.

Speed was Grant's mantra on May 17–18, since he felt Confederate morale ebbing. He ordered his troops to back the Confederates into Vicksburg and enclose their defenses with William Sherman's corps on the right, James B. McPherson's in the middle, and John McClernand's on the left. Grant sought to use his momentum to quickly defeat the Rebels by directly assaulting their defensive lines. Though a siege was an option from the beginning, his aggressive nature was not the only reason he ordered an assault. With the string of victories the Army of the Tennessee recently experienced, and the perception that the Confederate forces were disorganized, the Union soldiers needed a reason for a siege. Also, a siege required more material and men than his army currently had. Lastly, Grant was concerned that a siege would leave him vulnerable to an attack from the rear by Johnston's Confederate force. As darkness fell on them on May 18, the bulk of the Union forces took positions opposite the Confederate lines, investing the city. With full confidence of his army, Grant had pursued Pemberton to the outskirts of Vicksburg and was ready for his coup de grâce.

Just before noon of May 19, Grant ordered the Army of the Tennessee to launch their assault on the Confederate works protecting the isolated city. With little rest, preparation, and reconnaissance of the terrain, Union forces moved into attack position and waited for three artillery volleys, around 2 P.M., to signal a general charge on the Confederate lines. The lack of reconnaissance and unforgiving terrain hampered Grant's assault. Though the assault occurred across the entire Confederate line, the bloodiest fighting of the day was the Stockade Redan on the northeastern point of the Rebels' lines. Sherman's corps threatened the redan, but well-placed Confederate reinforcements pushed back the attackers before they could breach the defenses. Overall, Pemberton's defenses remained completely intact and repulsed Grant's assaults on May 19. The Union army sustained 932 casualties. While exact numbers for the Confederate losses are not known, it is estimated they suffered 200 casualties. That night the Army of the Tennessee went to camp for the first time during this campaign without victory. Morale in the Union ranks began to fall, while that of the Confederates improved. The first of Parker Hills's chapters researches the assaults on May 19 in detail while examining the various reasons Grant's first assault on Vicksburg failed.

During the following two days, May 20 and 21, both armies recovered from the previous assault and prepared for another attack. Grant was still determined to assault the Confederate lines and take Vicksburg as quickly as he could to avoid laying siege. Motivating Grant was the threat of Johnston's Army of Relief in his rear, and he did not want to unnecessarily pull from other important fronts the Union soldiers required for a siege. Grant planned that as soon as he took Vicksburg, he would send a detachment to capture Johnston. Instead of hurrying his men as he did on May 19, Grant took time to reconnoiter the terrain and position more of his men for a larger assault. Most important, they improved their earthworks, cleared the terrain in front of their positions, and built gun emplacements for their artillery. They hoped that improving the ground would ease their movements once they had launched their next assault. Additional emplacements would mean more guns available to help soften Confederate positions and support troops as they attacked. Despite the Confederates' best efforts, their constant bombardment of Union positions only slowed the Northerners' progress. With more cannons available, particularly rifled artillery, the Federals kept the Rebels occupied repairing damage to their earthworks. Lastly, Grant sent a brigade to cut off the last avenue for Confederates to escape on the Union left. Though Pemberton never considered escaping south from Vicksburg, the brigade did commit the Confederate commander to defending that point in his line and kept him from using those troops to reinforce other points. This commitment further closed avenues available for Pemberton to send and receive communications outside Vicksburg.

All along the line, the Army of the Tennessee pushed as close to the Confederate defenses as they could. Sherman's corps inched down the Graveyard Road and unlimbered nearly thirty cannons to shell the Stockade Redan. McPherson's corps deployed along the Jackson Road toward the 3rd Louisiana Redan and further south to connect with McClernand's right flank. Using the lessons he learned from the May 19 assault, McClernand moved men to threaten the 2nd Texas Lunette, which could pour flanking fire into any Union assault on the Railroad Redoubt. McClernand's men occupied a ridge immediately opposite the lunette and raked the Texans with artillery, knocking out two cannons and keeping them busy reinforcing and repairing their position.

Improving morale was also on Grant's agenda during the respite. He communicated with supply bases on the Yazoo to organize routes to the rear of the Union lines. On May 21, fresh supplies, particularly a sundry of food, arrived at their camp. As expected, food is a morale booster for men who had been marching constantly for nearly two months.

Pemberton spent the two days shoring his defenses by deepening the trenches and traversing them to limit casualties from the increasing artillery barrages. The improved Union positions and increased number of gun emplacements made these chores difficult. Adding to Pemberton's misery were subordinates such as John Bowen who vied to position his men in the defensive line to avoid their current assignment of fatigue duty. The commanding general was too busy improving his lines and repairing damage from Union barrages to reposition his troops with the much larger Union so close. Supplies also concerned Pemberton. Not only did he worry that Federal artillery could damage their armaments and foods, but he was also concerned that there were pro-Union elements within the Vicksburg population who could sabotage these vital supplies. Pemberton worked with what little was available to defend the most threatened position in the South.

Before sunrise on May 22, Union artillery softened the Confederate defenses in preparation for another general assault to start at 10 A.M. This time Union soldiers were better prepared with knowledge of the terrain, in many instances carrying ladders to scale steep embankments. Though Union forces had more time to prepare, the fighting proved more disorganized and vicious than the first assault had been. Sherman engaged only one regiment of the forty-one available to him primarily at the Stockade Redan, and McPherson did marginally better with five of his thirty regiments. The bloodiest fighting took place at the Railroad Redoubt at the center of the line. There McClernand's troops forced Confederates to abandon the Railroad Redoubt early in the day. Lacking reinforcements to exploit this breach, the Union forces could not hold it and were forced to retreat after a significant loss of men. Once again, Grant failed to move Pemberton and gain his quick victory. This time the casualties were greater for the Army of the Tennessee, which suffered 3,199 in total compared with the Army of Mississippi's estimated 500.

Hills's second chapter examines in detail the assault of May 22. Though all parts of the line receive attention, he most closely analyzes the fighting at the Railroad Redoubt, particularly blaming Grant for ignoring McClernand's request for support until it was too late. Juxtaposing this point of view is Steven E. Woodworth's chapter 3, which examines the fighting at the Railroad Redoubt from the Union perspective. Woodworth argues that Grant was justified in not supporting McClernand's breach because any reinforcement with the available troops could have been easily matched by Confederate reserves. One of those reserves was Waul's Texas Legion, the topic of Brandon Franke's chapter 4. Franke examines the engagement at the Railroad Redoubt from the perspective of these Texan reinforcements. Their tenacity in fighting prevented the Union soldiers from gaining a stronger foothold in the Confederate lines and, before the end of the day, forced the Northerners to abandon their gains.

Major events, such as these two assaults, garner unique responses. Charles D. Grear's chapter 5 examines the reactions of Midwesterners to the news of the first failures of Grant's Vicksburg campaign. Their responses differed for the usual political reasons. More important, the assaults symbolized a turning point in the Midwesterners' economic and social views of Grant's campaign to capture the Mississippi River and split the Confederacy in half.

Difficult terrain, strong defenses, and uncoordinated assaults twice kept Grant from moving Confederate defenders and gaining the quick victory he desired. Not wanting to risk more men in another assault, Grant finally conceded to laying siege to Vicksburg after May 22. Quelling his aggressive nature, Grant requested additional units and supplies from other fronts, and he reorganized Union forces to lay siege to the city. Though the second failed assault worsened Union morale, the troops' spirits improved when they realized there would not be another assault on the defensive works, at least for the next few weeks. On the other side of the lines, Confederate morale improved with the knowledge not only that their lines were strong but also that they had held their ground against an overwhelming force. The only hope for the surrounded Rebels at Vicksburg was that Johnston's Army of Relief would force Grant to lift the siege. This relief would never happen, and both sides settled into their respective lines for an unrelenting bombardment with no end in sight.

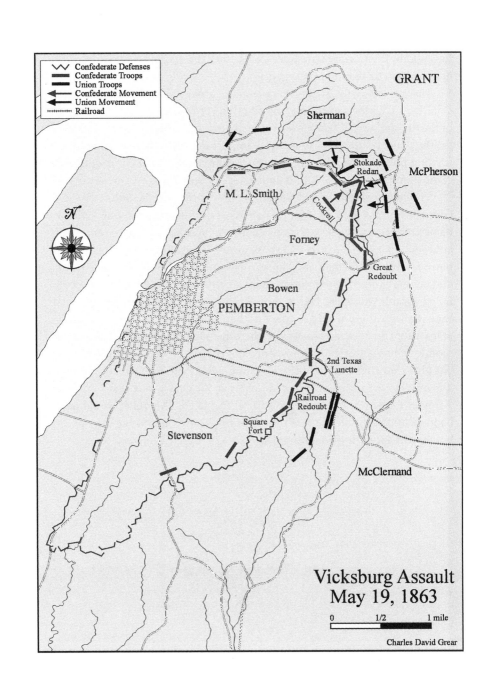

Confederate Defenses
Confederate Troops
Union Troops
Confederate Movement
Union Movement
Railroad

GRANT

Sherman

Stokade
Redan

McPherson

M. L. Smith

Cockrell

Forney

Great
Redoubt

Bowen

PEMBERTON

2nd Texas
Lunette

Railroad
Redoubt

Square
Fort

Stevenson

McClernand

Vicksburg Assault
May 19, 1863

0   1/2   1 mile

Charles David Grear

HASTE AND UNDERESTIMATION: MAY 19

J. Parker Hills

A dense blanket of smoke hung like a pall over the scab of raw earth surrounding Vicksburg, and the acrid smell of sulfur permeated the air. Downtown, a young mother viewed the afternoon fighting from the cupola balcony of the Warren County Courthouse, then preserved her thoughts in ink. "So twilight began falling over the scene—hushing to an occasional report the noise and uproar of the battle—falling softly and silently upon the river—separating us more and more from the raging passions surging around us—bringing only the heaven above us, and the small space of life we occupy, distinctly to our eyes." Soon afterward, the sylphlike new moon performed its cameo role, and then exited the darkened western stage. It was the 139th day of the year, Tuesday, May 19, 1863, and Vicksburg had been successfully isolated but unsuccessfully assailed.[1]

The vanguard of Ulysses Grant's Army of the Tennessee had arrived outside Vicksburg at 9:30 A.M. on Monday, May 18, 1863. It was an unusually hot day, and Grant rode forward through the haze of dust stirred by thousands of shuffling feet and hooves. Mounted on a bay mare, the general cut his way through the earthen fog and arrived at the fork of the Jackson and Countryman Roads, just under a mile east of the Vicksburg defenses. At the intersection, William T. Sherman waited with the lead elements of his Fifteenth Corps. At this critical junction, Grant instructed his trusted lieutenant to veer northwest on the Countryman Road to form the army's right. At the same time, word was sent back to James B. McPherson, commander of the Seventeenth Corps, whose men were still choking in the dust behind Sherman's troops on the Bridgeport and Jackson Roads. When McPherson arrived at the Countryman Road junction, he was ordered to continue east on the Jackson Road to constitute the army's center. A message was also sent several miles south to John A. McClernand, commander of the oversized Thirteenth Corps approaching Vicksburg on the Baldwin's Ferry Road. McClernand was instructed to continue west on that road to establish the army's left.[2]

Sherman snapped a salute to his chief and assigned a regiment to guard the road junction until McPherson's vanguard arrived. He then ordered Frank Blair's division to turn onto the Countryman Road, and orders were sent back to Frederick Steele's and James Tuttle's divisions of the Fifteenth Corps, instructing them to follow Blair's lead. Blair's gritty soldiers marched north for less than one-half mile and arrived at another road fork where the Graveyard Road ran west from the Countryman Road. Grant and Sherman were at the head of the column, so Blair was quickly ordered to turn west onto the Graveyard Road. As Blair's column made the left turn at 3:20 P.M., the head of the column came under fire from Confederate sharpshooters. Then, while the two generals schemed back at the road fork, a bullet whistled into the ever-present pack of straphangers around general officers and struck one of Sherman's engineers. Sherman and Grant paid little heed, and continued to puff their cigars and plan their movements. A messenger was rushed back to Steele, telling him that when he arrived at the intersection he was to continue northeast on the Countryman Road to make connection with Admiral David Dixon Porter's fleet in the Mississippi River. Tuttle's division, bringing up the rear, was to stop at the Countryman-Graveyard Roads intersection and encamp there to serve as the reserve division of the Fifteenth Corps.[3]

The cry of "On to Vicksburg!" crackled down the line like electricity, and Blair's men cautiously drove the Confederate skirmishers west on the Graveyard Road for another one-half mile. Finally, at 4 P.M., the redlegs of Company B, 1st Illinois Artillery, unlimbered one of their twelve-pounder howitzers, perched it on a knoll north of the road, and more for honor than effect, blasted a round at the Stockade Redan complex, nine hundred yards away. At the same time, Steele's division arrived at the Graveyard Road intersection and, per instructions, followed the Countryman Road for another two miles to Walnut Hills overlooking the Mississippi River. It was dusk when Tuttle's dust-covered reserve division began to stagger in, and the worn-out soldiers collapsed into camp at the assigned intersection.[4]

As darkness enveloped the hills of Vicksburg, the Seventeenth Corps began to arrive. In the lead was Thomas E. Ransom's brigade of John McArthur's two-brigade division. Ransom's troops trudged past the fork of the Jackson and Graveyard Roads and continued west for another quarter mile on the Jackson Road. To maintain contact with Sherman's left, Ransom turned right onto a dusty farm lane atop a ridgeline, and there his exhausted brigade dropped by the roadside three-fourths of a mile from the Confederate lines. John A. Logan's division of the Seventeenth Corps went into camp that night almost two miles from the Confederate lines, near the junction of the Jackson and Bridgeport Roads, to take advantage of the waters of Wren and Cook's Bayous. Two miles east of the Confederate defensive line the Bridgeport Road merged with the Jackson Road and took the latter road's name, and near this road junction John A. Logan's division of the Seventeenth Corps went into camp to take advantage of the waters of Wren and Cook's Bayous. Isaac Quinby's Seventeenth Corps division brought up the rear on the Bridgeport Road, and encamped behind Logan's soldiers.[5]

McClernand's Thirteenth Corps, after crossing the Big Black River early that morning, marched west on the Jackson Road. When the Thirteenth Corps arrived at the tiny community of Mt. Alban, Grant's orders were for McClernand to find "a parallel road within 3 miles of the direct road." McClernand obeyed and turned southwest at Mt. Alban, traveling three miles to Lanier's plantation. At Lanier's he turned his column northwest toward Vicksburg on the Baldwin's Ferry Road. By so doing, the Thirteenth Corps avoided having to rebuild a burned bridge over the Southern Railroad of Mississippi, one-half mile north of Mt. Alban, where the Jackson Road made an abrupt turn to the north. Just as important, Grant's orders turned McClernand off the Jackson Road and prevented the Thirteenth Corps from having to fall in behind Sherman's and McPherson's corps, which had approached Vicksburg from the east on the Bridgeport Road. Because of the six-mile round trip detour, three of McClernand's four divisions were strung out for miles along their circuitous route. Nightfall found the lead elements, Peter J. Osterhaus's and Andrew Jackson Smith's divisions, on the Baldwin's Ferry Road at Hatcher Bayou. There they enjoyed a wet camp just over two miles east of the Confederate lines. Eugene A. Carr's division was still a few miles to the rear and served as the reserve, while Alvin P. Hovey's division remained at Edwards and Big Black River to escort Champion Hill prisoners and guard the bridge crossings.[6]

The Federals were investing Vicksburg, and Grant later asserted in his *Memoirs* that his troops "had an abundance of food . . . but began to feel the want of bread [hardtack]." In reality, however, it was a hungry army that closed on Vicksburg on May 18, 1863. Sergeant Osborne Oldroyd of the 20th Ohio in Logan's division of the Seventeenth Corps wrote, "Our division made a long march today [May 18], and we have bivouacked for the night without supper, and with no prospect of breakfast, for our rations have been entirely exhausted." Private Stephen Rollins of the 45th Illinois in the same division wrote to his parents that on the morning of May 19, "[w]e started early, without rations." Captain Henry Nourse of the 55th Illinois in Blair's division of the Fifteenth Corps wrote that "our own division . . . had found but scanty gleaning during its march at the rear, and was now suffering for food." Lieutenant Charles Miller of the 76th Ohio of Steele's division of the Fifteenth Corps recalled that after his unit departed Jackson on May 16, "[t]he troops were short of rations and many went hungry. The country was bare of supplies after two armies had passed over it. It was very difficult especially for the officers to obtain food." Indeed, beans and bullets were on everyone's mind, and this was especially true with Sherman, who wore his logistical concerns like a weathered shawl. While the army was still in Louisiana, and even after it crossed the Mississippi, Sherman had expressed his fears over food and ammunition. Grant, too, recalled that his own "first anxiety was to secure a base of supplies on the Yazoo River above Vicksburg." He noted that "Sherman was equally anxious with myself. Our impatience led us to move in advance of the column and well up with the advanced skirmishers. . . . [T]he bullets of the enemy whistled by thick and fast for a short time." The path of the two generals took them another two miles along the Countryman Road ridge, and Grant recalled, "In a few minutes Sherman had the pleasure of looking down from the spot coveted so much by him the December before on the ground where his command had lain so helpless for offensive action." Here, from the heights of Walnut Hills, Sherman gazed to the northwest over the lowlands where he unsuccessfully assaulted the Confederates at Chickasaw Bayou the previous December. In the distance he could see the shimmery ribbon of the Yazoo River as it paralleled the horizon, and he could barely discern the ghostlike plumes of black smoke rising from the smokestacks of Admiral Porter's fleet. Just beneath the boats, at Johnson's burned plantation, Sherman could make out the mound of crates containing sustenance for Grant's army. On seeing that the essential supplies had been amassed by an intuitive Porter, Sherman experienced an epiphany, that is, the army's line of communication had been reestablished. He gleefully turned to Grant and said that though up to this minute he had felt no positive assurance of success, he now believed that this was one of the greatest campaigns in history. He blurted out that even if the city did not fall, this campaign was a complete and successful one. At this moment, Sherman was thinking tactically, that is, only about food and ammunition. He missed the strategic significance of the moment, that is, Porter's fleet on the Mississippi River blocked any Confederate flight westward, and Grant's army could thwart any escape attempt to the north, south, or east. Vicksburg was a doomed city.[7]

Grant left Sherman on the right flank of the army and inspected portions of his rudimentary lines until midnight on May 18. Then the general and his staff rode eastward for over a mile, following the Jackson Road to Dr. Cook's plantation at the junction of the roads to Bridgeport and Mt. Alban. There they spent the night in "an unpretentious farmhouse" that had been abandoned by the owner at the approach of the Federals. According to Sylvanus Cadwallader, an imbedded reporter from the *Chicago Times* who traveled with Grant, "there was not a pound of provisions of any kind to eat." Then, miraculously, just after midnight Cadwallader wrote, "some of the colored people caught, dressed and stewed a solitary turkey somehow left behind." Albert Richardson, an early Grant biographer, recalled this late-night repast when he wrote, "There was no salt, bread, nor vegetables, but the party ate eagerly, for they had fasted since daylight. It was nearly dawn when they went to bed with light hearts."[8]

Grant never mentioned his whereabouts on the next morning, Tuesday, May 19, but twelve-year-old Fred Grant, who accompanied his father on the campaign, recalled that his father "visited all parts of his command again, spending most of his time with McClernand . . . who was placed on the left." Sherman also wrote that Grant "was far on the left flank." Since Grant had ridden with Sherman and the Fifteenth Corps on the eighteenth, and had encamped with the Seventeenth Corps that night, it is only logical that he would ride to his left to see the disposition of the Thirteenth Corps the next morning. But Grant, who had gone to bed just before dawn, had almost four miles to ride to reach the Thirteenth Corps divisions at Hatcher Bayou, and these men departed their camps at dawn. Moreover, Grant probably did not see McClernand, who had sent a message to report his progress and to acknowledge the receipt of Grant's attack order, delivered by Clark B. Lagow, one of Grant's aides. But Grant had to know that aside from Blair's and Steele's divisions of the Fifteenth Corps, the rest of his troops had gone into camp well after dark the previous night, and that they were over two miles from the Confederate lines. Consequently, those units would still be moving into position on the morning of May 19, and it would take much of the day to move two Seventeenth Corps divisions and two Thirteenth Corps divisions to the front. Also, it would take time for the commanders to perform a reconnaissance of the ground to their front. Nevertheless, at 11:16 A.M. Grant issued his attack order, "Corps commanders will push forward rapidly, and gain as close positions as possible to the enemy's works until 2 o'clock P.M. At that hour they will fire three volleys of artillery from all the pieces in position. This will be the signal for a general charge of all the corps along the whole line." Strangely, no one seemed to realize that the signal to begin the attack—three cannon volleys—would serve to alert the defenders as well as the attackers.[9]

What was in Grant's mind when he decided to attack without having all of the divisions of two of his three maneuver corps in position? In his *Memoirs* he stated, "The enemy had been much demoralized by his defeats at Champion's Hill and the Big Black, and I believed he would not make much effort to hold Vicksburg." Although this statement was published in Grant's *Memoirs* in 1885, Grant obviously believed it at Vicksburg in 1863, because on the morning of the nineteenth he sent a message to Admiral Porter, requesting him to "run down and throw shell in just back of the city" to aid the army and "to demoralize an already badly beaten enemy." There appears to be no doubt that Grant believed Pemberton's men would not offer stiff resistance. Adam Badeau, Grant's approved biographer, wrote, "The troops were buoyant with success and eager for an assault, and their commander believed himself justified in an attempt to carry the works by storm." Badeau's statement that the men were "eager for an assault" must be questioned. When the men of the 48th Ohio learned of the planned attack, the unit historians wrote, "The news was received by the regiment in a quiet and serious manner, and the suspense until 2 o'clock was somewhat like that of the culprit awaiting the hour of execution."[10]

Nevertheless, there was another factor for Grant's decision to attack on May 19. The sweltering, almost suffocating, climate of Mississippi in late spring and early summer weighed heavily on Grant's mind when he wrote that he wanted to possess Vicksburg "before the season was too far advanced for campaigning in this latitude." In his *Memoirs* Grant recalled that during the war with Mexico, "[i]t was very important to get the army away from Vera Cruz as soon as possible, in order to avoid the yellow fever, or vomito, which usually visits that city early in the year, and is very fatal to persons not acclimated." Even Robert E. Lee, who had served in Mexico with Grant, believed that the Mississippi climate would affect Grant's army. When Lee was pressed by the Confederate government to send support to Vicksburg from Virginia, he wrote to Secretary of War James A. Seddon on May 10, saying, "The climate of June will force the enemy to retire."[11]

Regardless of the reason for the Vicksburg assault of May 19, 1863, it began at 2 P.M. Time was not taken to perform a proper reconnaissance, position troops, establish a mission statement, or prepare an organized, coordinated plan of attack. A modern Grant biographer stated it succinctly—the attack was "too hasty, too improvised, and based on too much optimism."[12]

On the Union right, Blair's division of William T. Sherman's Fifteenth Corps attacked the Stockade Redan complex and bore the brunt of the action there. On Blair's right the crescent-shaped 27th Louisiana Lunette, perched to the northwest of the Stockade Redan, was the objective of General Hugh Ewing's brigade. While two of Ewing's regiments, the 30th and 37th Ohio, became mired in the bottom of Mint Spring Bayou, the 47th Ohio and 4th West Virginia continued forward. These regiments, after crossing Mint Spring

Bayou, had to climb a nearly vertical seventy-foot slope in front of the lunette. Sergeant Joseph A. Saunier, the regimental historian of the 47th Ohio wrote:

> The deadly iron and lead thinned our ranks, but we kept on dashing forward and when we gained the foot of the hill we sprang up its sides with a wild Yankee yell and gained the crest of the hill, where we charged the enemy's works. Our flag was planted on the outside of the enemy's works—we could do no more. A large part of the 47th occupied the ditch, but could not effect an entrance into the fort. The enemy, secure in its fortifications, lighted the fuses of large bomb shells, and threw or rolled them down into the ditch upon the men. ... After a few minutes of this firing at such close range, we drew back to the shelter of the hill and lay down on our faces. Here we had some protection from the withering fire of the enemy. Now the crying of the wounded for water was heard. We lay under the hill, and could not withdraw from our perilous position near the ditch until after dark.[13]

For two and a half hours, the close-quarter fighting at the 27th Louisiana Lunette continued until darkness ended the carnage. In the lunette's ditch, Confederates captured the 47th Ohio's Federal flag after shooting the color-bearer in the hand. The sergeant swore that he could not bring the flag off "because of the dead men lying on it." Despite, or perhaps because of, the color-sergeant's lamentations the commander of the 47th, Colonel Augustus C. Parry, "cursed the soldier, called him a coward, and threatened to cut off his head with a sword." The regiment apparently shared the colonel's sentiment, because the historian recorded that "this was the first and last flag ever lost by the 47th Ohio during its term of over four years, and we know that no one deplored the loss of that flag more than the members of the regiment. The writer would have brought out that flag or he would have left his bones bleaching on Southern soil."[14]

In Blair's center, north of the Graveyard Road, Giles Smith's brigade maneuvered through a deep ravine to form in line atop a ridge three hundred yards northeast of the Stockade Redan. Confederate small arms fire soon whizzed into the blue formation, causing Smith to order the 8th Missouri to fall out and provide covering fire for his other four regiments. While the Missourians blazed away, from left to right Smith's attacking line included the Regular Army soldiers of the 1st Battalion, 13th U.S. Infantry, the 116th Illinois, 113th Illinois, and 6th Missouri. Despite receiving heavy fire, these regiments descended into the ravine of Mint Spring Bayou, and worked their way through the freshly trampled cornstalks of farmer Adam Lynd's fields. The corn crop had recently stood waist-high, but in the past few hours the green promise of nourishment had been stomped into a lifeless parchment carpet by Sherman's skirmishers. Fifty yards below the membrane of stalks, at the very point where the gradient rendered the field too steep to plow, the attackers kicked down a worm rail fence placed there to keep livestock in the ravine and out of the fields. Another few yards past the fence stood a wall of abatis, or felled trees with sharpened branches facing the attacker. The menacing lancets were strung with a network of telegraph wire to snare any attacker who was either brave or foolish enough to enter the maze. Finally, the highly erodible soil was pitted with sinkholes, which were filled with spikes and covered with grass to create booby traps, or tiger pits.[15]

Soldiers moving across uneven ground will flow like water, and the Federal formation quickly dissolved as each member subconsciously took the path of least resistance. Despite their training not to cluster, as the soldiers moved downhill they merged, like two-lane highway traffic with one lane closed, and created a human traffic jam at the base of the draw, only eighty yards northeast of the Stockade Redan. This area at the foot of the draw was a beaten, or kill zone, covered by fire from the Stockade Redan and the 27th Louisiana Lunette. Those who made it through the beaten zone then had to climb the steep slope out of the ravine. In the process, the 250-man Regular Army battalion lost seven of its twelve officers and sixty-four of its enlisted men. Their attack finally stalled at the ditch on the north face of the Stockade Redan.[16]

Blair's left brigade, commanded by T. Kilby Smith, attacked on both sides of the Graveyard Road. The three regiments south of the road, the 55th Illinois, 54th Ohio, and 57th Ohio, lost their formation when they came under fire, and the soldiers quickly went to ground behind the eastern ridge of the Glass Bayou watershed, 150 yards from the Stockade Redan. The two regiments north of the road, the 83rd Indiana and 127th Illinois, had no such cover and, along with Giles Smith's men, had to fight their way through the Mint Spring Bayou ravine to the defilade area fronting the Stockade Redan, where the assault ended.[17]

While Blair attacked on the left, Sherman ordered Frederick Steele's division on the far Union right to move into position and dig in on Indian Mound Ridge, the northern watershed of Mint Spring Bayou. Although this anchored the Union right, the action for two of Steele's three brigades was light, with only John Thayer's Iowa brigade, consisting of the 4th, 9th, 26th, and 30th Iowa, coming under serious fire from the 26th Louisiana Redoubt, 640 yards northwest of the Stockade Redan. Therefore, Steele's total division casualties were 9 dead and 55 wounded, compared with Blair's 120 dead, 485 wounded, and 8 missing. Sherman's third division, James Tuttle's, was in reserve, thus Tuttle suffered only 4 men killed and 26 wounded. At day's end the official losses for the Fifteenth Corps were 134 killed, 571 wounded, and 8 missing, for a total of 713.[18]

In the Union center, only Ransom's brigade of John McArthur's division of McPherson's Seventeenth Corps was in position to attack at the appointed 2 P.M. hour. But, as has happened since time immemorial, someone failed to get the word, and the Irishmen of the 17th Wisconsin attacked seventeen minutes early at a point just south of Green's Redan. The commander of the 95th Illinois, Thomas W. Humphrey, had aligned his regiment on the left of the Irish badgers, and he felt honor-bound to protect his sister regiment. Colonel Humphrey quickly stepped his men off to cover the left flank of the 17th, even though the other three regiments in Ransom's brigade, the 14th Wisconsin, 11th Illinois, and 72nd Illinois, were not in position. After traversing the steep and deep ravine of the north fork of Glass Bayou, the two attacking regiments came under galling small arms fire from the 37th and 38th Mississippi regiments. Yet somehow, the assailants managed to advance to within one hundred yards of the Confederate line, only to be enfiladed by cannon fire from the 3rd Louisiana Redan on the Jackson Road, one thousand yards to the south. The beleaguered Federals had no choice but to hunker down and dig in. Soon Colonel Humphrey received a note from General Ransom saying, "You have done well, nobly." The two regiments eventually pulled back at 4 A.M. on May 20. McArthur's division suffered 124 casualties—14 killed and 110 wounded—including Colonel Humphrey, who was shot in the foot, but still remained with his men.[19]

While Ransom's two regiments were engaged, John Logan's division of the Seventeenth Corps was still shuffling into position on the Jackson Road on Ransom's left. This road crowned the highest ridge in the area, and Logan's lead brigade, John E. Smith's, marched to a white house perched atop a small hill 375 yards east of the 3rd Louisiana Redan. The structure was a nine-room Creole cottage known as Wexford Lodge, and the matron of the house, Adeline Shirley, stubbornly remained in her home despite the firing. Adeline's daughter, Alice, who was not at home at the time, later described what her mother saw when J. E. Smith's men approached:

> The Confederates, knowing that they must soon retreat behind their fortifications at Vicksburg, began preparations by destroying what they could outside, and burned all the houses in the vicinity; but my mother's persistent refusal to go out of hers, and her determination to prevent its destruction, delayed its being set on fire until the Federals made their appearance on the hills to the east of us. The poor

fellow who was appointed to do the work, while holding the ball of blazing cotton to the corner of the house, was struck by a bullet of the pursuing vanguard, and crept away under the shelter of some planks, where he died alone. His body was found the next day and was buried under the corner of the house.[20]

Logan's division suffered no casualties, and south of the "White House," as Wexford Lodge became known, George B. Boomer's brigade of Quinby's division moved into position eight hundred yards in front of the Great Redoubt, a rectangular fort one hundred yards south of the Jackson Road. As in Logan's division, there was no attack at this point in the line, but Boomer had two killed and three wounded. The final casualty count in the three divisions of the Seventeenth Corps, which was the center of the Union line on May 19, totaled 129, with 16 killed and 113 wounded.[21]

Grant assigned the Union left to John A. McClernand's Thirteenth Corps, and at first light General McClernand and his staff rode westward from their campground at Hatcher Bayou and followed the Baldwin's Ferry Road to the spacious yard of the white, gabled Ferguson house on Durden Ridge. From that vantage point McClernand overlooked the Durden Creek bottom. Peering over the crest of Two Mile Ridge, almost three-quarters of a mile distant, he scanned the western horizon with his binoculars and discerned an earthwork almost a mile and a quarter away, where the railroad cut sliced through the Confederate line. He also saw that the Baldwin's Ferry Road was blocked three hundred yards northeast of the railroad by a second earthwork. Finally, one thousand yards southwest of the railroad was a huge earthwork. To approach this formidable line, McClernand could see that his troops would have to travel cross-country by descending eighty feet into the scrub-choked hollow of Durden Creek; wade through the four-hundred-yard-wide swampy floodplain; and climb eighty feet to the crest of Two Mile Ridge. What he could not see was that another, lower ridge separated Two Mile Ridge from the Confederate lines, so after crossing Two Mile Ridge his troops would have to precipitously drop sixty feet into the narrow valley of an intermittent stream, Two Mile Branch, and climb the lower sixty-foot-high ridge, the plateau of which was one hundred yards wide in places. Moreover, the plateau of the hidden ridge was a beaten zone, because it was only four hundred yards from the Confederate lines and could be raked with artillery and small arms fire. Then, after racing across the beaten zone, the troops would have to descend eighty feet into an abatis-choked ravine bisected by another intermittent stream. The final challenge of the twenty-one-hundred-yard attack from Durden Ridge to the objective was a steep eighty-foot climb to the Confederate fortifications. But because Two Mile Ridge masked the lower ridge and ravines west of it, McClernand would not see the intervening ground until after his men reached the Two Mile Ridge crest. A very successful businessman once said, "Time spent in reconnaissance is seldom wasted."[22]

While McClernand studied through his binoculars, behind him A. J. Smith's and Osterhaus's divisions moved out of their Hatcher Bayou camps at 5 A.M. Osterhaus's division was in the advance, and the trailing Osterhaus rode gingerly in the saddle due to a flesh wound received on his inner left thigh because of an exploding caisson during the fight at the Big Black River two days previously. The column marched westward for one mile to Durden Ridge, and Captain F. H. Mason of the 42nd Ohio, serving as an aide to McClernand, remembered:

> As the column climbed up out of the ravine it turned a curve in the road near a large white house, which afterwards became the center of a village of field hospitals. Rounding this curve, the great line of defenses was suddenly disclosed. For three miles to the right and left, along the whole front, the sharp cut crest of the Rebel fortifications formed the horizon line. . . . A moment after there was a puff of white smoke from the distant parapet, and a shell, singing and shrieking through the air, crashed through a locust tree in front of the house and buried itself in the earth. The gun that had fired it was two miles away, but in the clear morning air it seemed less than a mile.[23]

By 6:30 A.M. Osterhaus's and A. J. Smith's divisions had arrived on Durden Ridge, but the ridge crest was only 850 yards long, and space for deployment was limited. Osterhaus turned Albert L. Lee's brigade, consisting of the 118th Illinois, 49th and 69th Indiana, 7th Kentucky, and 120th Ohio, south on the ridge to form a line almost two hundred yards long, with Lee's right flank anchored on the Baldwin's Ferry Road. Daniel W. Lindsey's brigade, consisting of the 22nd Kentucky and the 16th, 42nd, and 114th Ohio, arrived later that morning, and Osterhaus placed these troops in reserve in a cornfield behind Lee's men. A. J. Smith arrived and turned north on the ridge to crowd his two brigades, William J. Landrum's, consisting of the 77th, 97th, and 130th Illinois, 19th Kentucky, 48th Ohio, and Stephen G. Burbridge's four regiments, the 16th and 67th Indiana, 83rd Ohio, and 23rd Wisconsin, into a 350-yard space between the Baldwin's Ferry Road and the railroad. Burbridge anchored his left flank on the Baldwin's Ferry Road, and Landrum anchored his right flank on the railroad. McClernand's other two divisions, Carr's and Hovey's, were still miles to the rear.[24]

The 1st Wisconsin Light Artillery, known as "The Bean Hole Battery" due to their method of baking their beloved army beans in pits of coals, unlimbered the right gun of their six twenty-pounder Parrott rifles "in the road just in front of a large white house that became a hospital, and sent a few shells into the line of rebel infantry, and they retired beyond the crest." The time was 10 A.M.[25]

When McClernand's rifled guns opened fire from Durden Ridge, the infantry moved forward. Confederate skirmishers from the 2nd Texas were quickly driven out of the Durden Creek hollow, and after an uphill scramble, the Federals reached the crest of Two Mile Ridge. Then, at a range of nine hundred yards, the Confederate cannon opened fire at the Federals atop the ridge. The two divisions sought cover by abandoning the ridge crest and tumbling down the western side of the ridge, down into the maze of ravines of Two Mile Branch.[26]

Sometime before noon, McClernand received Grant's order for a 2 P.M. attack on the Confederate lines. At the appointed time the eighteen rifled guns of the Thirteenth Corps, which had moved forward to Two Mile Ridge, opened fire and the infantry advanced. The historians of the 48th Ohio in Landrum's brigade recalled what happened as they advanced out of Two Mile Branch:

> Promptly at the hour the signal-gun was fired, and the order came, "Forward, 48th!" We started up the hill, and on reaching the summit we were greeted with shot and shell from the rebel forts; but without faltering, on we went, down into the next ravine, through brush and over fallen trees. Arriving at the foot of a hill, we continued up the narrow valley under the guns of the fort, and drove the rebel outposts into their fortifications, when a halt was ordered, to allow the troops to join us on the left. By the time they made the connection the sun was setting in the west. Our opportunity for taking Vicksburg that day had passed, and we bivouacked for the night.[27]

On McClernand's left, Lee's brigade entered a deep ravine, four hundred yards east of the Square Fort. Following the flow of the terrain, the flank regiments closed on the center, forming a confused mass. Colonel Marcus Spiegel, commanding the 120th Ohio, described the action in a letter to his wife:

> I never saw shot, shell, grape and bullets fly thicker in my life and yet I had but four men wounded and my men stood and kept their line as on dress parade while on the charge and during the hottest.

Brigadier General Lee . . . came up to me and said, "Spiegel by God you are a man after my own heart; you are doing bully and your men are the bravest I ever saw." . . . I am struck by a piece of shell on my left knee which knocked the skin off, bruised it some and makes it a little painful. . . . General Lee was wounded by the same shell badly; he had to leave the field. I am sorry; he is a brave and gallant officer and a gentleman.

Casualties for Osterhaus's division were 2 men killed and 63 wounded, while A. J. Smith's division had 5 killed and 30 wounded, for a total of 100 casualties in the Thirteenth Corps, with 7 killed and 93 wounded.[28]

While time and terrain greatly hampered Grant's assault of May 19, the Confederate reaction to the assault has to be considered. Earthworks and terrain aside, the successful defense at the only threatened portion of the line, the Stockade Redan complex, was due to the Confederate reserves. The purpose of a reserve force is twofold: for the prolongation and renewal of the combat and for use in case of unforeseen events. General John C. Pemberton, commander of the Confederate forces in Vicksburg, wisely planned his reserves for an unforeseen threat to his line. In his report, Pemberton stated why he assigned that critical mission to two units: General John S. Bowen's small division and Colonel Thomas N. Waul's Texas Legion:

> To man the entire line, I was able to bring into the trenches about eighteen thousand five hundred muskets, but it was absolutely necessary to keep a reserve always ready to re-enforce any point heavily threatened. It became indispensable, therefore, to reduce the number in the trenches to the minimum capable of holding them until a reserve could come to their aid. It was also necessary that the reserve should be composed of troops among the best and most reliable. Accordingly, Bowen's division (about 2,400) and Waul's Texas Legion (about 500) were designated for that purpose, thus reducing the force in the trenches to little over 15,500 men. . . . [O]n the evening of the 19th [the Legion] was transferred to [Carter L.] Stevenson's division.[29]

Normally, the army commander retains control of the reserves, but on May 19, Pemberton showed great confidence in Bowen when he wrote to his junior division commander: "Your discretion is relied upon to move where the assault is most heavy near you, and within aid of you. Look well to this, and make such disposition as an emergency requires. I am on the line, looking to our general interests. Do you so, too." Bowen did not disappoint his commander. He quickly alerted Colonel Francis M. Cockrell's tough Missouri brigade, which was near the city cemetery, three-quarters of a mile from the Stockade Redan complex. The Missourians were positioned to cover the Confederate left and left center. General Martin E. Green's brigade was positioned in the rear of General John C. Moore's brigade, near the Confederate supply depot in the Confederate center. Waul's legionnaires were placed behind General Stephen D. Lee's brigade near the Railroad Redoubt at the Confederate right center. For command and control, Bowen made his headquarters about halfway between the Jackson Road and the railroad, in the valley of Stout's Bayou east of the Confederate supply depot. The locations of the reserve forces were designed to use interior lines to reach critical points, and were based on the three avenues of approach that Grant's army had used on the previous day to reach the Vicksburg defenses: the Graveyard Road, the Jackson Road, and the Baldwin's Ferry Road. When the Confederate left and left center were hit by Blair's and Steele's divisions, four of Cockrell's five regiments raced to the trenches to stiffen the line. Such is the advantage of interior lines and a well-considered reserve force.[30]

On May 19, the total butcher's bill for Grant's three corps was 157 killed, 777 wounded, and 8 missing, for 942 total reported casualties. Confederate casualty reports are incomplete with 8 killed, 62 wounded, and no missing, but the total losses can be estimated at around 200. Strangely, after suffering almost one thousand Federal casualties, Grant biographer Badeau wrote that "night had overtaken the national forces before they were really in a condition to obey the order of Grant." This begs the question that if the troops were not "in a condition to obey the order of Grant," why was the order given? It is a commander's responsibility to do his best to ascertain the condition and position of the enemy and to know the condition and position of his own troops.[31]

By Civil War standards, Grant's losses on May 19, 1863, seem small, but by today's standards a loss of almost one thousand soldiers would be considered horrendous. The public, the media, and the Congress would demand answers, and the commander held accountable. Nevertheless, this was not necessarily so in 1863—a time when news traveled slowly and a victory overshadowed the cost. In fact, Grant did not mention his casualties in his after-action report, nor did anyone ask. After all, it was evident that Vicksburg was doomed and that Union forces would open the Mississippi for commercial navigation. Even as late as 1881, Badeau estimated the losses on the nineteenth to be at "fewer than five hundred; of these about one hundred were killed or severely wounded." Moreover, in his 1885 *Memoirs*, Grant again ignored the casualty figure for May 19, but he did attempt to justify the attack when he wrote, "It resulted in securing more advanced positions for all our troops where they were fully covered from the fire of the enemy." Yet, the "advanced positions" could and should have been attained through reconnaissance and infiltration, sparing the army the trauma of a frontal assault. The Chinese general Sun Tzu wrote that the commander should "[p]robe the enemy and learn where his strength is abundant and where deficient." In the final analysis, Grant struck when he should have probed.[32]

Notes

1. Mary Ann Loughborough, *My Cave Life in Vicksburg* (1864; repr., Wilmington, NC: Broadfoot Publishing Company, 1989), 46.

2. U.S. War Department, *The War of the Rebellion: A Compilation of the Official Records of the Union and Confederate Armies*, 128 vols. (Washington, DC: Government Printing Office, 1880–1901), series 1, vol. 24, pt. 1: 54, 641, 648–49, 755; ibid., pt. 2: 60, 256, 266. Hereinafter cited as *OR*. All references are to series 1 unless otherwise indicated. S. H. M. Byers, *With Fire and Sword* (New York: Neale Publishing Company, 1911), 74; Jean Edward Smith, *Grant* (New York: Simon and Schuster, 2001), 303; U. S. Grant, *Personal Memoirs of U. S. Grant*, 2 vols. (New York: Charles L. Webster and Company, 1885), 1: 527; William T. Sherman, *Memoirs of General W. T. Sherman*, 2 vols. (New York: Charles L. Webster and Company, 1892), 1: 352; Adam Badeau, *Military History of Ulysses S. Grant*, 3 vols. (New York: D. Appleton and Company, 1885), 1: 281; Reuben B. Scott, *The History of the 67th Regiment, Indiana Infantry Volunteers* (Bedford, IN: Herald Book and Job Print, 1892), 34; Francis Vinton Greene, *The Mississippi* (New York: Charles Scribner's Sons, 1882), 166–67; Kenneth P. Williams, *Lincoln Finds a General*, 4 vols. (New York: MacMillan Company, 1956), 4: 384–85; Edwin C. Bearss, *The Campaign for Vicksburg*, 3 vols. (Dayton: Morningside House, 1986), 3: 745–46; Warren E. Grabau, *Ninety-Eight Days, A Geographer's View of the Vicksburg Campaign* (Knoxville: University of Tennessee Press, 2000), 347–48; James H. Wilson, "A Staff Officer's Journal of the Vicksburg Campaign, April 30 to July 4, 1863," *Journal of the Military Service Institution of the United States* 43 (1908), 263; Lucien B. Crooker, Henry S. Nourse, John G. Brown, *The Story of the Fifty-Fifth Regiment, Illinois Volunteer Infantry* (Clinton, MA: W. J. Coulter, 1887), 234; Joseph Stockton, *War Diary* (Chicago: John T. Stockton, 1910), 15; John Quincy Adams Campbell, *The Union Must Stand*, edited by Mark Grimsley and Todd D. Miller (Knoxville: University of Tennessee Press, 2000), 98–99; W. S. Morris, L. D. Hartwell, J. B. Kuykendall, *History 31st Regiment Illinois Volunteers* (repr., Herrin, IL: Crossfire Press, 1991), 66–67; Ira Blanchard, *I Marched with Sherman: Civil War Memoirs of the 20th Illinois Volunteer Infantry* (San Francisco: J. D. Huff and Company, 1992), 94; Seth J. Wells, *The Siege of Vicksburg from the Diary of Seth J. Wells* (Detroit: William H. Rowe, Publisher, 1915), 65. Today, the Jackson and Countryman Roads intersection is Culkin Road and Sherman Avenue, fifty yards west of Hwy 61.

3. *OR*, vol. 24, pt. 1: 641, 648–49, 755, 760, 763, 765, 770; ibid., pt. 2: 256, 266–67; Williams, *Lincoln Finds a General*, 4: 385; Grant, *Personal Memoirs*, 1: 527–28; Sherman, *Memoirs*, 1: 352–53; Bearss, *Campaign for Vicksburg*, 3: 746, 749; Grabau, *Ninety-Eight Days*, 348; Wilson, "Staff Officer's Journal," 263; John S. Kountz, *History of the 37th Regiment, O.V.V.I.* (Toledo, OH: Montgomery and Vrooman Printers, 1889), 21; Joseph A. Saunier, *A History of the Forty-Seventh Regiment, Ohio Veteran Volunteer*

Infantry (Hillsboro, OH: Lyle Printing Company, 1903), 142–43; Crooker, Nourse, Brown, *Fifty-Fifth Illinois*, 234; Charles Dana Miller, *The Struggle for the Life of the Republic*, edited by Stewart Bennett and Barbara Tillery (Kent, OH: Kent State University Press, 2004), 95; A. A. Hoehling, *Vicksburg: 47 Days of Siege* (repr., New York: Fairfax Press, 1991), 22–23; David W. Reed, *Campaigns and Battles of the Twelfth Regiment Iowa Veteran Volunteer Infantry* (Evanston, IL: Library of Congress, 1903), 121–22. The roads forming the intersection of Graveyard and Countryman Roads are today Sherman Avenue and Howe Lane.

4. *OR*, vol. 24, pt. 2: 251, 256–57, 263, 266–67, 276–77; Sherman, *Memoirs*, 1: 352–53; Bearss, *Campaign for Vicksburg*, 3: 749–51; Charles A. Willison, *Reminiscences of a Boy's Service with the 76th Ohio* (Menasha, WI: George Banta Publishing Company, 1908), 54; Charles E. Affeld diary, May 18, 1863, Vicksburg National Military Park Archives, Vicksburg, MS. The first Union cannon shot was fired from an unmarked knoll on Sherman Loop, ninety yards north of Grant Avenue in Vicksburg National Military Park. Wilson, "Staff Officer's Journal," 263; Saunier, *Forty-Seventh Ohio*, 142; Crooker, Nourse, Brown, *Fifty-Fifth Illinois*, 234; Miller, *Struggle for the Life of the Republic*, 95; Stockton, *War Diary*, 15.

5. *OR*, vol. 24, pt. 1: 641, 648–49; ibid., pt. 2: 60, 67, 297, 301; Grant, *Personal Memoirs*, 1: 528–29; Sherman, *Memoirs*, 1: 353; Badeau, *Military History of Ulysses S. Grant*, 1: 282–83, 303; Greene, *Mississippi*, 166–67; Bearss, *Campaign for Vicksburg*, 2: 632–33; ibid., 3: 720–21, 751, 757, 805–6; Grabau, *Ninety-Eight Days*, 357–58; Campbell, *Union Must Stand*, 98–99; Edmund Newsome, *Experience in the War of the Great Rebellion* (Carbondale, IL: Edmund Newsome, Publisher, 1880), 49; Myron B. Loop, *The Long Road Home: Ten Thousand Miles through the Confederacy with the 68th Ohio*, edited by Richard A. Baumgartner (Huntington, WV: Blue Acorn Press, 2006), 93; Blanchard, *I Marched with Sherman*, 94; Wales W. Wood, *A History of the Ninety-Fifth Regiment Illinois Infantry Volunteers* (Chicago: Tribune Company's Book and Job Printing Office, 1865), 73; Alonzo L. Brown, *History of the Fourth Regiment of Minnesota Infantry Volunteers during the Great Rebellion, 1861–1865* (St. Paul, MN: Pioneer Press, 1892), 211. Ransom, by turning off the Jackson Road onto modern Kolb Road, formed the right flank of the Seventeenth Corps. The junction of the Jackson Road (modern Mt. Alban Road) and Bridgeport Road (modern Freetown Road or Culkin Road) is in the modern community of Culkin, about one-half mile east of highway 61. Ransom's brigade had not been involved in any of the previous battles of the campaign. It escorted one of Grant's supply trains from Grand Gulf, having left on May 13 to arrive at Champion Hill on May 16, after the fighting had ended. McArthur was with the other brigade of his division, William Hall's, which was en route to Vicksburg after helping garrison the Grand Gulf supply base, and did not arrive at Vicksburg until May 22. William W. Belknap, Loren S. Tyler, *History of the Fifteenth Regiment, Iowa Veteran Volunteer Infantry* (Keokuk, IA: R. B. Ogden and Son, 1887), 255–56.

6. *OR*, vol. 24, pt. 1: 153, 596, 617; ibid., pt. 2: 17, 33, 46; ibid., pt. 3: 324; Grant, *Personal Memoirs*, 1: 528–29; Sherman, *Memoirs*, 1: 353; Wilson, "Staff Officer's Journal," 261–63; Badeau, *Military History of Ulysses S. Grant*, 1: 282–83, 303; Greene, *Mississippi*, 166–67; Bearss, *Campaign for Vicksburg*, 3: 743–45, 758, 790; Grabau, *Ninety-Eight Days*, 351; Dan Webster and Don C. Cameron, *History of the First Wisconsin Battery Light Artillery* (Washington, DC: National Tribune Company, 1907), 147; W. H. Bentley, *History of the 77th Illinois Volunteer Infantry* (Peoria, IL: Edward

Hine, Printer, 1883), 144–45; Isaac H. Elliott, *History of the Thirty-Third Regiment Illinois Veteran Volunteer Infantry in the Civil War* (Gibson City, IL: Press of the Gibson Courier, 1902), 194; Mary B. Townsend, *Yankee Warhorse: A Biography of Major General Peter Osterhaus* (Columbia, MO: University of Missouri Press, 2010), 106; Frank Holcomb Mason, *Forty Second Ohio Infantry: A History of the Organization and Services of that Regiment in the War of the Rebellion* (Cleveland: Cobb, Andrews and Company, 1876), 216; William Wiley, *The Civil War Diary of a Common Soldier*, edited by Terrence J. Winschel (Baton Rouge: Louisiana State University Press, 2001), 49; Virgil Gilman Way and Isaac Hughes Elliott, *History of the Thirty-Third Regiment Illinois Veteran Volunteer Infantry in the Civil War* (Gibson City, IL: Published by the Association, 1902), 41–43; Thomas B. Marshall, *History of the Eighty-Third Ohio Volunteer Infantry* (Cincinnati: Gibson and Perin Company, 1913), 83; John A. Bering and Thomas Montgomery, *History of the Forty-Eighth Ohio Vet. Vol. Inf.* (Hillsboro, OH: Highland News Office, 1880), 84; Scott, *67th Indiana*, 34–35; Regimental Association, *History of the Forty-Sixth Regiment Indiana Volunteer Infantry* (Logansport, IN: Press of Wilson, Humphreys and Company, 1888), 62–64. The Hatcher Bayou campsite is at the intersection of Paxton Road with Old Highway 27. This is also the site of Camp Fisk, the primary exchange point in 1865 for Union prisoners captured in the Western theater.

7. Grant, *Personal Memoirs*, 1: 527–30; Osborn H. Oldroyd, *A Soldier's Story of the Siege of Vicksburg from the Diary of Osborn H. Oldroyd* (Springfield, IL: Published for the author, 1885), 27; Wells, *Siege of Vicksburg*, 65; Crooker, Nourse, Brown, *Fifty-Fifth Illinois*, 234–35; Miller, *Struggle for the Life of the Republic*, 95; Lydia Minturn Post, *Soldiers' Letters from Camp, Battle-Field and Prison* (New York: Bunce and Huntington, 1865), 267; David D. Porter, *The Naval History of the Civil War* (New York: Sherman Publishing Company, 1886), 320; Badeau, *Military History of Ulysses S. Grant*, 1: 281; Albert D. Richardson, *Personal History of Ulysses S. Grant* (Hartford, CT: American Publishing Company, 1868), 321; Frederic D. Grant, "Gen. Ulysses S. Grant: His Son's Memories of Him in the Field," *National Tribune*, February 3, 1887, 1; Lloyd Lewis, *Sherman: Fighting Prophet* (New York: Harcourt, Brace, and Company, 1932), 277; James M. McPherson, *Battle Cry of Freedom: The Civil War Era* (New York: Oxford University Press, 1988), 631; Stanley P. Hirshson, *The White Tecumseh: A Biography of General William T. Sherman* (New York: John Wiley and Sons, 1997), 155; Edward D. Mansfield, *Popular and Authentic Lives of Ulysses S. Grant and Schuyler Colfax* (Cincinnati: R. W. Carroll and Company, 1868), 208; Williams, *Lincoln Finds a General*, 4: 384–85; Allan Nevins, *The War for the Union*, 8 vols. (New York: Charles Scribner's Sons, 1971) 3: 61; Samuel Carter III, *The Final Fortress: The Campaign for Vicksburg 1862–1863* (repr., Wilmington, NC: Broadfoot Publishing Company, 1988), 208; Smith, *Grant*, 252; William L. Shea and Terrence J. Winschel, *Vicksburg Is the Key: The Struggle for the Mississippi River* (Lincoln: University of Nebraska Press, 2003), 142–43; Michael B. Ballard, *Vicksburg: The Campaign That Opened the Mississippi* (Chapel Hill, NC: University of North Carolina Press, 2004), 324; Edwin C. Bearss and J. Parker Hills, *Receding Tide: Vicksburg and Gettysburg* (Washington, DC: National Geographic Society, 2010), 233. Sherman's "epiphany point" is on Sherman Avenue at the intersection with Gentleman Avenue, 1.8 miles past the Graveyard Road (modern Howe Lane) intersection. The crest of the ridge has been leveled and is now a sports field.

8. F. D. Grant, "Gen. Ulysses S. Grant," 1; Sylvanus Cadwallader, *Three Years with Grant*, edited by Benjamin P. Thomas (repr., Lincoln: University of Nebraska Press, 1996), vi, 87; Richardson, *History of Ulysses S. Grant*, 322; Wilson, "Staff Officer's Journal," 263; Calvin D. Cowles, *Atlas to Accompany the Official Records of the Union and Confederate Armies* (Washington, DC: Government Printing Office, 1891–95), plate 36 (1). Dr. Cook's home was at the site of today's Culkin Academy building.

9. F. D. Grant, "Gen. Ulysses S. Grant," 1; John Russell Young, *Around the World with General Grant*, 2 vols. (New York: American News Company, 1879), 2: 615; *OR*, vol. 24, pt. 1: 54; 153–54; ibid., pt. 3: 327, 329; Samuel Rockwell Reed, *The Vicksburg Campaign, and the Battles about Chattanooga: An Historical Review* (Cincinnati: Robert Clarke and Company, 1882), 101; Grant, *Personal Memoirs*, 1: 529; John Y. Simon, editor, *The Papers of Ulysses S. Grant*, 31 vols. (Carbondale: Southern Illinois University Press, 1967–2009), 8: 237; Wilson, "Staff Officer's Journal," 263; Bearss, *Campaign for Vicksburg*, 3: 761; Grabau, *Ninety-Eight Days*, 356; Reed, *Vicksburg Campaign, and the Battles about Chattanooga*, 99.

10. Grant, *Personal Memoirs*, 1: 529; *OR*, vol. 24, pt. 3: 326–27; Reed, *Vicksburg Campaign, and the Battles about Chattanooga*, 100; Smith, *Grant*, 475, 622; Badeau, *Military History of Ulysses S. Grant*, 1: 301; Bering and Montgomery, *Forty-Eighth Ohio*, 86.

11. *OR*, vol. 24, pt. 1: 55; ibid., vol. 25, pt. 2: 790; Grant, *Personal Memoirs*, 1: 129–30; Nevins, *War for the Union*, 8: 66; Bearss and Hills, *Receding Tide*, 161, 233.

12. Brooks D. Simpson, *Ulysses S. Grant: Triumph over Adversity* (Boston: Houghton Mifflin Company, 2000), 203.

13. Bearss, *Campaign for Vicksburg*, 3: 764–65; W. P. Gault, *Ohio at Vicksburg* (Columbus: Ohio Vicksburg Battlefield Commission, 1906), 100; A. S. Abrams, *A Full and Detailed History of the Siege of Vicksburg* (Atlanta: Intelligencer Steam Power Presses, 1863), 31; Kountz, *History of the 37th Regiment, O.V.V.I.*, 21; Saunier, *Forty-Seventh Ohio*, 144; Bearss and Hills, *Receding Tide*, 236. The Stockade Redan complex was designed to protect the Graveyard Road avenue of approach into Vicksburg. The three-fort complex consisted of the 27th Louisiana Lunette 100 yards northwest of the road, the Stockade Redan tangential to the road, and Green's Redan 185 yards southwest of the road.

14. Saunier, *Forty-Seventh Ohio*, 145; *OR*, vol. 24, pt. 2: 153, 259.

15. *OR*, vol. 24, pt. 1: 756; ibid., pt. 2: 264, 267; Badeau, *Military History of Ulysses S. Grant*, 1: 301–2; Bearss, *Campaign for Vicksburg*, 3: 761; Terrence J. Winschel, *Triumph and Defeat: The Vicksburg Campaign* (Mason City, IA: Savas Publishing Company, 1999), 120; Ballard, *Campaign That Opened the Mississippi*, 328.

16. *OR*, vol. 24, pt. 2: 263–64; Bearss, *Campaign for Vicksburg*, 3: 762–63; Sherman, *Memoirs*, 1: 352; Winschel, *Triumph and Defeat*, 126; Headquarters, Department of the Army, *Field Manual No. 3–22.68, Crew-Served Machine Guns 5.56-mm and 7.62-mm* (Washington, DC: U.S. Government Printing Office, July 21, 2006), 5-2; Bearss and Hills, *Receding Tide*, 234–35.

17. *OR*, vol. 24, pt. 2: 267–68, 271, 274, 276; Crooker, Nourse, Brown, *Fifty-Fifth Illinois*, 235–36; Sherman, *Memoirs*, 1: 352; Bearss, *Campaign for Vicksburg*, 3: 762; Bearss and Hills, *Receding Tide*, 234.

18. *OR*, vol. 24, pt. 1: 756, 760, 763; ibid., pt. 2: 159, 251; Bearss, *Campaign for Vicksburg*, 3: 765, 774–76; Ballard; *Campaign That Opened the Mississippi*, 330–32;

Kevin J. Dougherty, *Leadership Lessons: The Campaigns for Vicksburg, 1862–1863* (Philadelphia: Casemate, 2011), 155.

19. *OR*, vol. 24, pt. 1: 755; ibid., pt. 2: 159, 297, 299, 300, 376; ibid., pt. 3: 326; Badeau, *Military History of Ulysses S. Grant*, 1: 303; Wood, *Ninety-Fifth Illinois*, 73–75; Post, *Soldiers' Letters*, 204–5, 222; Bearss, *Campaign for Vicksburg*, 3: 746, 757, 769–70, 778; Grabau, *Ninety-Eight Days*, 351; Greene, *Mississippi*, 169–70; Ballard, *Campaign That Opened the Mississippi*, 331; Bearss and Hills, *Receding Tide*, 236–37.

20. *OR*, vol. 24, pt. 1: 709, 713, 718, 755; ibid., pt. 2: 60, 67, 159, 206, 292; ibid., pt. 3: 326; Wood, *Ninety-Fifth Illinois*, 74; Wells, *Siege of Vicksburg*, 65–66; Bearss, *Campaign for Vicksburg*, 3: 741, 770, 778, 782; 795–96; W. H. Tunnard, *A Southern Record: The History of the Third Regiment, Louisiana Infantry* (Baton Rouge: Printed for the author, 1866), 236–37; Alice Shirley, *Alice Shirley and the Story of Wexford Lodge*, edited by Terrence J. Winschel (Ft. Washington, PA: Eastern National, 1993), 16; Parker Hills, *Art of Commemoration: Vicksburg National Military Park* (Vicksburg, MS: Vicksburg Convention and Visitors Bureau, 2012), 10. The Shirley House, built about 1837, is the only wartime structure remaining in Vicksburg National Military Park.

21. *OR*, vol. 24, pt. 2: 60, 159; Bearss, *Campaign for Vicksburg*, 3: 757–58.

22. *OR*, vol. 24, pt. 1: 153; ibid., pt. 2: 17–18, 33; Bearss, *Campaign for Vicksburg*, 3: 758–59; Grabau, *Ninety-Eight Days*, 356–57; Townsend, *Yankee Warhorse*, 106–7; Richard L. Kiper, *Major General John Alexander McClernand: Politician in Uniform* (Kent, OH: Kent State University Press, 1999), 251. Sir MacPherson Robertson quote is at http://www.mauicroquetclub.org/people/MacPhersonRobertson.htm, accessed July 19, 2015. In his report, McClernand confused Two Mile Creek with Durden Creek. The earthwork at the railroad cut was the Railroad Redoubt; the 2nd Texas Lunette was on the Baldwin's Ferry Road, and southwest of the railroad was the Square Fort. In the late 1960s Interstate 20 was constructed, cutting through the area between Two Mile Ridge and the lower ridge 460 yards to the west. Today Union Avenue in Vicksburg National Military Park runs along the lower ridge. Porter's Chapel Road follows the crest of Two Mile Ridge; John Marsden, Tomorrow, *When the War Began* (Boston: Houghton Mifflin Company, 1995), 73.

23. *OR*, vol. 24, pt. 1: 152, 153, 592, 617; ibid., pt. 2: 17, 46; ibid., pt. 3: 324; Bearss, *Campaign for Vicksburg*, 2: 362, 666; ibid., 3: 743–45, 757–58, 857; Grabau, *Ninety-Eight Days*, 351; Bentley, *77th Illinois Volunteer*, 141–42, 144–45; Townsend, *Yankee Warhorse*, 3, 7, 106; Mason, *Forty-Second Ohio*, 214, 218. The "large white house" Mason refers to is the Ferguson house, today known as "Sarata," on Durden Ridge at the curve in the historic Baldwin's Ferry Road (Old Highway 27). Captain Mason was not an artilleryman and his range estimate was exaggerated, as the Confederate gun was just over a mile away.

24. *OR*, vol. 24, pt. 1: 153; ibid., pt. 2: 17, 18, 27; Bearss, *Campaign for Vicksburg*, 3: 758–59; Grabau, *Ninety-Eight Days*, 356–57; Townsend, *Yankee Warhorse*, 107.

25. Webster and Cameron, *First Wisconsin Battery Light Artillery*, 32, 96, 147. The historians of the 1st Wisconsin Battery recalled: "In the garden the 'husky cannoneers' noted a bed of onions rapidly wilting under the morning sun, probed, found resistance, and unearthed a large box of silverware; but before they could divvy the provost guard took possession."

26. *OR*, vol. 24, pt.1: 153–54; ibid., pt. 2: 17–18, 27, 229–33, 387; Marshall, *Eighty-Third Ohio*, 83–84; Bering and Montgomery, *Forty-Eighth Ohio*, 85–86; Scott, *67th*

Indiana, 35–36; Marcus Spiegel, *Your True Marcus: The Civil War Letters of a Jewish Colonel*, edited by Frank L. Byrne and Jean Powers Soman (Kent, OH: Kent State University Press, 1985), 281; Joseph E. Chance, *The Second Texas Infantry from Shiloh to Vicksburg* (Austin, TX: Eakin Press, 1984), 104; Bearss, *Campaign for Vicksburg*, 3: 759; Grabau, *Ninety-Eight Days*, 357.

27. *OR*, vol. 24, pt. 1: 153–54; ibid., pt. 2: 18, 230–31; Bearss, *Campaign for Vicksburg*, 3: 771; Grabau, *Ninety-Eight Days*, 357; Bering and Montgomery, *Forty-Eighth Ohio*, 86.

28. *OR*, vol. 24, pt. 1: 154; ibid., pt. 2: 17, 230–31; Bearss, *Campaign for Vicksburg*, 3: 771–72; Grabau, *Ninety-Eight Days*, 357; Spiegel, *Civil War Letters of a Jewish Colonel*, 281.

29. Karl von Clausewitz, *On War*, translated by O. J. Matthijs Jolles (Washington, DC: Combat Forces Press, 1943), 155; *OR*, vol. 24, pt. 1: 273; U.S. Congress, *Report of General Joseph E. Johnston together with Lieut. General Pemberton's Report* (Richmond: R. M. Smith, Public Printer, 1864), 49–50; Samuel H. Lockett, "The Defense of Vicksburg," *Battles and Leaders of the Civil War*, edited by Robert U. Johnson and Clarence C. Buell, 4 vols. (New York: Century Company, 1887), 3: 488.

30. *OR*, vol. 24, pt. 2: 414, 420; ibid., pt. 3: 892–93; Bearss, *Campaign for Vicksburg*, 3: 737, 761; Ephraim McD. Anderson, *Memoirs: Historical and Personal; Including the Campaigns of the First Missouri Confederate Brigade* (repr., Dayton: Morningside Bookshop, 1988), 328–29; R. S. Bevier, *History of the First and Second Missouri Confederate Brigades, 1861–1865* (St. Louis: Bryan, Brand, and Company, 1879), 199, 201; Phillip Thomas Tucker, *The Forgotten Stonewall of the West: Major General John Stevens Bowen* (Macon, GA: Mercer University Press, 1997), 295. The Confederate supply depot was on Stout's Bayou, 850 yards northwest of the 2nd Texas Lunette.

31. *OR*, vol. 24, pt. 1: 159; Bearss, *Campaign for Vicksburg*, 3: 773–74; Badeau, *Military History of Ulysses S. Grant*, 1: 303; Headquarters, Department of the Army, *Field Manual No. 100–5, Operations* (Washington, DC: Government Printing Office, June 1993), 11-2.

32. *OR*, vol. 24, pt. 1: 159; ibid., pt. 2: 159; Bearss, *Campaign for Vicksburg*, 3: 773–74; Ballard, *Campaign That Opened the Mississippi*, 332; Michael B. Ballard, *Grant at Vicksburg: The General and the Siege* (Carbondale: Southern Illinois University Press, 2013), 94; Smith, *Grant*, 252; Badeau, *Military History of Ulysses S. Grant*, 1: 303–4; Richardson, *History of Ulysses S. Grant*, 323; Grant, *Personal Memoirs*, 1: 529; Sun Tzu, *The Art of War*, translated by Samuel B. Griffith (New York: Oxford University Press, 1963), 100; Alexander Pope, "An Essay on Criticism," (London, 1709; Cambridge: Cambridge University Press, 2013).

2

FAILURE AND SCAPEGOAT: MAY 22

J. Parker Hills

A n aging Ulysses Grant nestled in a deck chair on the fantail of the new iron steamer, SS *City of Tokio*, all the while puffing his omnipresent cigar. It was nighttime on the Pacific, and each time he drew on his Havana the glow would momentarily reveal his timeworn face. Despite the calm seas of that September evening in 1879, Julia Grant had retired early, still sporting the avocado pallor of a landsman after two years at sea. But the general, despite the twenty cigars he smoked each day, had proven throughout the voyage that he was impervious to the effects of mal de mer. Then, as soon as his temperate wife was out of sight, the general gratefully accepted a shimmering snifter of cognac from his opportunistic *New York Herald* interviewer. Finally, armed with both smoke and drink, the old warrior was comfortable and could relish his freedom from the glass bell of command. Always one to embrace a long evening chat with a friend, he began to speak freely. Nevertheless, just after midnight Grant fell silent and gazed aft, across the effervescent trail of lacy foam. After a few moments of reflection, he turned and softly said, "I don't think there is one of my campaigns with which I have not some fault to find, and which, as I see now, I could not have improved, except perhaps Vicksburg. I do not see how I could have improved that."[1]

The Vicksburg Campaign was without question Grant's masterpiece. But was Grant correct—was there no room for improvement? Of course, any accomplishment of great merit can be, and almost certainly will be, second-guessed by those of an investigative nature. Sometimes the motive is as simple, and as brazen, as jealousy, for after all is said and done, it is infinitely easier to criticize than to accomplish. But not all motives are so dark, and there are lessons to be learned by dissecting both successes and failures. So, in the spirit of learning, and in total agreement with the U.S. Army that the Vicksburg Campaign remains "the most brilliant campaign ever fought on American soil," an examination is offered of one facet of Grant's masterpiece— the assault on Vicksburg of Friday, May 22, 1863.[2]

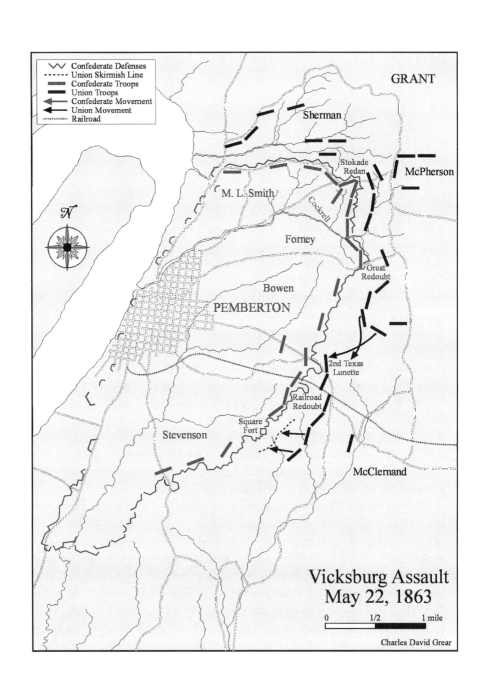

Vicksburg Assault
May 22, 1863

Confederate Defenses
Union Skirmish Line
Confederate Troops
Union Troops
Confederate Movement
Union Movement
Railroad

GRANT

Sherman

McPherson

Stokade
Redan

M. L. Smith

Cockrell

Forney

Great
Redoubt

Bowen

PEMBERTON

2nd Texas
Lunette

Railroad
Redoubt

Square
Fort

Stevenson

McClernand

0   1/2   1 mile

Charles David Grear

On Tuesday, May 19, Grant's attack on Vicksburg had failed at a cost of almost one thousand Federal soldiers. Yet this hasty assault was merely a precursor to a more deliberate and much more costly attack a mere sixty-eight hours later. The question has to be asked: Why was there a second attempt against a heavily fortified position with interior lines and a strong reserve, and upon which the first assault was repulsed? In Grant's report of July 6, 1863, he wrote that after his Tuesday attempt he spent Wednesday and Thursday reestablishing his line of communication; then he "determined to make another effort to carry Vicksburg by assault" on Friday, May 22. Grant stated his reasons: He thought an assault would succeed; he was concerned that Joseph E. Johnston would attack him from the rear; he was concerned about the summer climate; he wished to prevent reinforcements being sent to him that were needed elsewhere; and he believed that his troops wanted another chance to take Vicksburg. In 1885, when Grant discussed the Vicksburg Campaign in his *Memoirs* he repeated his concerns about Johnston, and he repeated his desire to avoid reinforcements being sent to Vicksburg. He also added a few more thoughts on the matter in a later chapter when he wrote, "There was no telling what the casualties might be among Northern troops working and living in trenches, drinking surface water filtered through rich vegetation, under a tropical sun." Then he wrote, "But the first consideration of all was the troops believed they could carry the works in their front, and would not have worked so patiently in the trenches if they had not been allowed to try." One must question this "first consideration," because Grant would have the reader believe that after the first failed attack, his soldiers were eager to make a second attack against well-fortified and well-defended positions. In contrast to Grant's statement, Charles E. Wilcox of the 33rd Illinois wrote in his diary that they

> [g]ot the orders to charge upon the enemy's works at 10 o'clock in the morning. Our whole line is to charge. Our Brigade and regimental officers in the Brigade look sad when talking of these orders, and are opposed to them as a general thing. . . . [M]y heart is much depressed when meditating upon our duty for the morrow. The men don't want to charge and yet they say they will do it when ordered.[3]

Regardless of the mood of the soldiers, Grant's explanatory statement is actually a thinly veiled attempt to avoid the responsibility for ordering the attack. The attack, Grant said, was ordered because the troops wanted it; thus, he had to let them try. In other words, the troops made him do it. But commanders do not poll the troops to determine what they want. To command is to accept that, as the troops would say, "You are no longer one of us." The commander is surrounded with a deference unlike that accorded to other officers, and this form of respect is unique in that it isolates. This insulation, or loneliness, is the price that one who controls the lives of soldiers must pay, that is, deciding when they eat or sleep, when they receive reward or punishment, and sometimes whether they live or die. Moreover, those soldiers must trust that their commander has the wisdom, integrity, humanity, courage, and discipline to do what is right. What the soldier may or may not desire should not be a consideration in the commander's decision-making, for the soldier is trained to think and act tactically, not strategically, and the soldier does not command. Simply stated, the military is not a democracy and soldiers do not vote on command decisions. After Grant's death in 1885, John Russell Young said of him: "He was free from the rhetoric of emotion." Yet when Grant opted for a second assault based on what he felt the troops wanted, as opposed to what experience had shown him, it was an emotional act. Grant succumbed to the impression of the senses, rather than to the forces of logic. Accomplishing the ultimate goal may mean hardship for the troops, and may require actions that go contrary to their wishes, but such is the responsibility and loneliness of command.[4]

William T. Sherman wrote that Grant called his three corps commanders together on Wednesday, May 20, saying, "We compared notes, and agreed that the assault of the day before had failed, by reason of the natural strength of the position, and because we were forced by the nature of the ground to limit our attacks to the strongest points of the enemy's line, vis., where the principal roads entered the city." Of course, this is precisely how the Confederate defenses were designed—the bastions were positioned to guard the avenues of approach, and at these points the terrain channelized the enemy into beaten zones that were heavily covered by artillery and small arms fire. Sherman, therefore, stated the obvious. Nevertheless, the meeting resulted "in orders from General Grant for us to make all possible preparations for a renewed assault on the 22d, simultaneously, at 10 A.M." Anyone can make a mistake, and the uncoordinated attack of May 19 was certainly a mistake. But to repeat the same mistake twice is irresponsible.[5]

John McClernand, Grant's senior corps commander, did not agree with the decision to attack a second time. McClernand was the maverick of Grant's corps commanders due to his lack of formal military education, a position of which he was painfully aware. He knew he was not a member of Grant's inner circle—and he resented it. Seven months earlier, Secretary of the Navy Gideon Welles accurately described McClernand as a man who "dreads association with any West Point general—considers them too self-sufficient, pedantic and impracticable." It certainly was no secret in the ranks of soldiers, sailors, and politicians that McClernand and Grant were as oil is to water, and there was no love lost between McClernand and other West Point officers. In contrast, corps commanders Sherman and James B. McPherson were very close to Grant. After all, they were fellow West Point graduates and all three men were Ohio-born. But, ironically, it was McClernand, the nonprofessional soldier, who saw the recklessness of another frontal assault on Vicksburg, and after the meeting on May 20, he dutifully wrote to Grant and expressed his concerns. He reminded Grant of the strength of the Confederate fortifications, saying "the whole line [is] in a very commanding position." He said that he had information that the defense was in depth in his front, and that he did not think that the position could be carried with the army's extended lines. He advised "a change of the plan of attack and the concentration of our forces on some particular point or points. Otherwise, perhaps, a siege becomes the only alternative." Advice from a political general apparently did not sit well with Grant, for he did not give McClernand the courtesy of a response.[6]

On the afternoon of May 20, despite his concerns, McClernand went ahead with preparations for Grant's ordered attack. He surveyed the area to his front, and quickly saw that the key position in his sector was the ground between the Railroad Redoubt and the 2nd Texas Lunette. These two fortifications provided mutual support, and an attacking force on either of the bastions would be hit with a devastating flanking fire from its sister fort. While the railroad followed a narrow man-made cut to the redoubt, the Baldwin's Ferry Road led to the lunette along ground that, while not flat, was much less convoluted than the ravines and canebrakes in front of the redoubt and north of the lunette. McClernand, therefore, ordered A. J. Smith to move his division from his position behind a low ridge about four hundred yards southeast of the lunette, follow the Baldwin's Ferry Road ridge, and seize ground that would provide better fields of fire for keeping the Confederates pinned down, thus reducing the threat of enfilading fire.[7]

Due to a gap that existed between McClernand's corps right and McPherson's corps left, McClernand advised McPherson of A. J. Smith's planned movement, and asked him to assist, "should the enemy move out to attack my right flank." As Smith's advance progressed, McClernand sent Grant a message to advise that he was pressing up to the enemy's works, and he noted that his fellow corps commanders were doing little. "I hear nothing on the right or center," he wrote to Grant. After Smith secured the desired ground northeast of the 2nd Texas Lunette, McClernand sent another message to Grant, advising him that "General Smith is within some hundred yards of the works. He says McPherson should advance on his right." A. J. Smith, a West Point graduate, could clearly see two commanding three-hundred-foot knolls on the crest of a ridge 350 yards to his right. In Smith's mind, the occupation of these knolls would both cover his right flank and serve as excellent jumping-off points for the May 22 attack.[8]

McClernand's note that Sherman and McPherson seemed to be inactive, coupled with his advice to Grant on how to position McPherson's corps, apparently hit a nerve with Grant. Grant had established his headquarters in the Federal center, near McPherson's headquarters, where the young general was tucked away behind a hillock 750 yards east of the 3rd Louisiana Redan. Grant was positioned at Mt. Ararat, just 250 yards east of McPherson, on a prominence on the south side of the Jackson Road. At 405 feet in elevation, the appropriately named Mt. Ararat was the highest point in the area, and with its panoramic view it was an excellent point for command and control, and for signaling commanders on both ends of the Federal line. From this lofty vantage point Grant testily replied to McClernand's message, which said that "Smith is within some hundred yards of the works," by tersely saying, "McPherson is within fifty yards of the main fort and can see Genl. Smith's men." This message withheld important information, it was disingenuous, and it was a case of one-upmanship in defense of Grant's protégé, McPherson. Grant falsely claimed that McPherson had advanced closer to the enemy than A. J. Smith, when in reality neither Sherman nor McPherson reported any advances that day, other than getting the artillery into position and moving some troops up to support the guns. But Sherman's closest guns were 350 yards east of the Stockade Redan near the Graveyard Road. McPherson's closest guns on his right flank were 300 yards from the Confederate lines, while those in his center straddled the Jackson Road and were 400 yards from the defenses. McPherson's left flank troops, George B. Boomer's brigade of Isaac F. Quinby's division, were a distant 800 yards east of the Great Redoubt. Quinby's other two brigades, commanded by John B. Sanborn and Samuel A. Holmes, were still en route to Vicksburg from the Big Black River. Thus, McPherson had only Boomer's brigade available on his left flank, and that brigade had too much ground to cover to extend to A. J. Smith's right. McClernand should have been advised of this fact. Moreover, McPherson was nowhere near being "within fifty yards of the main fort," with the possible exception of a handful of skirmishers who had moved in front of the 3rd Louisiana Redan. McClernand had shown initiative in gaining ground in preparation for the planned assault, and Grant, rather than congratulate and provide support for his Thirteenth Corps commander, petulantly chose to rebuff, and even worse, misinform him.[9]

After Grant's unseemly gamesmanship with McClernand, he advised McPherson that if he intended to advance any of his Seventeenth Corps units, he should send word to Sherman so that Sherman's left could cover

McPherson's right. Of course, this is precisely what McClernand had asked of McPherson. But there was no need to contact Sherman, because McPherson had no plans for a move forward. Instead, he chose to extend Boomer's men to his left, but still seven hundred yards from McClernand's right flank. Fortunately for A. J. Smith, although his right flank was uncovered during and after his forward movement on May 20, he was successful in the seizure of the coveted ground and the Confederates did not contest his advance. By late afternoon Smith's line had extended 300 yards to the north, with the 67th Indiana occupying a knoll 280 yards northeast of the 2nd Texas Lunette. The 300-foot elevation of this knoll was twenty feet higher than the lunette, giving the Hoosiers the advantage of plunging fire on the Texans.[10]

The events of May 20 indicated that the spirit of cooperation in the Army of the Tennessee, that is, unity of command, was strained at best, and broken at worst. In fact, late on May 19, Sherman had written to his wife after the first unsuccessful attack, saying, "Grant is off to the left with McClernand, who *did not* press his attack as he should." Sherman, on the far Union right, could not possibly have seen what happened in McClernand's sector on the far Union left. The distance between Sherman's attack on the Union right and McClernand's attack on the Union left was over two and one-half miles, and between those two flanks the four-hundred-foot-high Jackson Road ridge prevented line of sight. Thus Sherman irresponsibly passed on secondhand information, and regardless of the source, it was nothing more than petty gossip. When McClernand advanced A. J. Smith's division, Grant should have put an end to the backbiting and pettiness, not participate in it. But he failed to set aside his dislike of McClernand, the nonprofessional soldier, and in so doing he failed to ensure that he and his commanders worked seamlessly for the accomplishment of the mission. This failure would bear bitter fruit on May 22.[11]

At 6 P.M. on Thursday, May 21, Grant issued the attack order for 10 A.M. the next morning. Despite the experiences of the first assault and the meeting with his corps commanders to compare notes and discuss the attack, Grant's order provided only the most rudimentary guidance:

A simultaneous attack will be made to-morrow, at 10 o'clock A.M. by all the Army Corps of this Army. During to-day Army Corps Commanders will have examined all practicable routes over which troops could possibly pass. They will get in position all the Artillery possible and gain all the ground they can with their Infantry and skirmishers. At an early hour in the morning a vigerous attack will be commenced by Artillery and skirmishers. . . . Promptly at the hour designated all will start at quick time, with bayonets fixed, and march immediately upon the enemy, without firing a gun until the outer works are carried.

The order was poorly written even if spelling were not considered. Grant's commanders were not given specific objectives; a main effort was not identified; there was no clear fire support plan; and finally, there was no plan to exploit any success. Unlike the Confederate commander in Vicksburg, John Pemberton, who had organized a highly professional and mobile reserve, Grant did not plan for a reserve force to take advantage of a possible breakthrough.[12]

Before dawn on May 22, the Union preparatory fire, which included 220 cannon of Grant's army and 100 naval guns of Porter's ironclads, blasted the predawn darkness into daylight. Hot iron screeched into the hunkered-down Confederates manning the trenches and onto the hapless civilians holed up in Vicksburg. On the Union right, Frank Blair's twenty-seven guns focused on the Stockade Redan complex. In the center, John A. Logan's fourteen pieces tore up the earth of the 3rd Louisiana Redan, while McPherson's other thirty guns, including two monster thirty-pounder Parrott rifles, tore into the Great Redoubt. On the Federal left, forty-five cannon, three of which were thirty-pounder Parrott rifles, ripped their shells into the 2nd Texas Lunette, the Railroad Redoubt, and the Square Fort. The barrage hammered the Confederate lines for over four hours, lasting until 10 A.M. Since all Federal pocket watches were synchronized with Grant's, precisely at 10 A.M. the guns fell silent. An acrid shroud of smoke settled over the battlefield, then, as one Southern soldier recalled, the Federals sprang "from the bowels of the earth."[13]

On the Union right, Sherman, having watched his men struggle in the ravines during the assault of May 19, decided to take the easier ground and attack in a column formation down the Graveyard Road. He issued orders to his commanders on May 21:

> Blair's and [James M.] Tuttle's divisions will assault along the main [Graveyard] road, by the flank, the head of the column preceded by a selected, or volunteer, storming party of about 150 men. . . . [Frederick] Steele's division will in like manner attack, by any route he may select, the one to the front of [John M.] Thayer [26th Louisiana Redoubt] being suggested. . . . Each column will attack by the watch, and not depend on signals.

Sherman had unwittingly adopted McClernand's suggestion by attacking in column along the Graveyard Road, that is, he decided to punch the enemy with his fist, rather than poke at him with his finger. However, Sherman's plan sent his men directly into a carefully planned beaten zone. This kill zone was in front of the Stockade Redan where the narrow dirt road made a slight curve westward and debouched from a fifteen-foot-deep cut. This spot in the road was covered by fire from the Stockade Redan, 120 yards to the attackers' front, from Green's Redan, 225 yards to the attackers' left, and from the 27th Louisiana Lunette, 240 yards to the attackers' right. It was a perfect kill zone because any enemy attacking on the road would be channelized into a narrow column by the steep earthen walls of the cut, and then it would be a simple matter of shooting down the vanguard, then the second rank, and any other rank brave or foolish enough to follow.[14]

While the artillery boomed on Friday morning, May 22, Sherman positioned himself at a point 390 yards east of the Stockade Redan on the lee side of a protective ridge. He peered at his objective though the smoke and dust, then nervously glanced down at his watch. At 10 o'clock there was a sudden, tense hush, and an eerie calm settled over the blanket of smoke. Then came the sound of feet shuffling in the dust. It was the 150 volunteers of the "Forlorn Hope" double-timing down the road immediately to Sherman's right. In a matter of seconds, the forty-yard-long column entered the hundred-yard-long cut in the road, with the volunteers carrying planks and ladders for crossing the Stockade Redan's ditch and for scaling the parapet. In less than two minutes the party emerged from the cut, and Sherman recalled that a hidden double rank of Confederates suddenly arose and "poured on the head of the column a terrific fire. It halted, wavered, and sought cover." In the Stockade Redan the grim foot soldiers of the 36th Mississippi of Louis Hébert's brigade and the 1st and 5th Missouri of Francis M. Cockrell's reserve brigade were shocked at the horrific results of their fire. One Missourian noted that "the destruction among the federal ranks was fearful." Of the 150 Forlorn Hope volunteers, 19 were killed and 34 were wounded.[15]

Within minutes Blair's men charged down the Graveyard Road in a column of fours at trail arms. The 30th Ohio of Hugh Ewing's brigade was at the head of the long, blue, snakelike column, followed by the 37th Ohio, then the 47th Ohio, and finally the 4th West Virginia. As the vanguard entered the beaten zone the incoming fire ripped into them. The commander of the 30th Ohio, George H. Hildt, recalled that "on account of the severe fire of the enemy, [the road cut] soon became impassable—choked with dead and wounded, preventing our further advance in force." Men went down four at a time, until the 30th Ohio could stand no more. The next regiment to enter the cut was the 37th Ohio, but these buckeyes, on entering the beaten zone and seeing the bloody and writhing bodies of their fellow Ohioans, threw themselves down and hugged the ground. Generals Ewing and Blair were in the midst of the carnage, and the two commanders unsuccessfully screamed orders in an effort to motivate the soldiers. They then resorted to cajoling the prone troops, but the terrified men refused to budge. Blair, a fiery man, quickly realized that due to the jammed road cut he had no option but to turn the last two regiments, the 47th Ohio and 4th West Virginia, to the left and off the road. By doing so, in less than 100 yards the two regiments were able to take cover behind a ridge 150 yards south of the road and east of the redan. Sherman's thrust had been parried. Blair's other two brigades, Giles Smith's and T. Kilby Smith's, soon followed Ewing's troops and filed to the left, past the 47th Ohio and 4th West Virginia, which were hunkered down behind the crest of the ridge, and slowly worked their way south and downward into the ravine of Glass Bayou. Here Blair hoped that the two brigades might attempt an assault on the only untested work of the Stockade Redan complex—Green's Redan. But the difficult terrain and abatis delayed these brigades until early afternoon, when they finally reached a point three hundred yards southeast of the redan. James M. Tuttle's reserve division, almost one-quarter mile to the rear on the Graveyard Road, stood in ranks all morning, the men uneasily awaiting the attack order that never came. Steele's division on the far Union right did not get into position to attack the 26th Louisiana Redoubt until midafternoon; thus, these Fifteenth Corps troops did not participate in the morning assault. Sherman wrote, "[F]or about two hours, we had a severe and bloody battle, but at every point we were repulsed." In reality, the action on the Graveyard Road was over in about twenty minutes, and Sherman's pitiful attack had been reduced to a storming party of 150 brave volunteers and one unfortunate regiment—the 30th Ohio—less than five hundred soldiers.[16]

In the center of Grant's line in the Seventeenth Corps, only Thomas E. G. Ransom's brigade of John McArthur's two-brigade division was in attack position on McPherson's right flank. Division commander McArthur was with his other brigade, William Hall's, and was en route to Vicksburg from Warrenton after having helped garrison Grant's supply base at Grand Gulf. Two of Ransom's regiments had been stung badly on the May 19 assault, so he ordered his men to descend quietly into the concealment of the abatis in Glass Bayou. By around 11 A.M. his troops were at a point sixty yards from the Confederate line. Ransom then looked to his right before issuing the attack order, and was bewildered to discover that his right flank was uncovered, and that the fire from Green's Redan could enfilade his entire line. Discretion being the better part of valor, Ransom chose not to attack until he could receive support on his right. This support would eventually come from Giles Smith's Fifteenth Corps brigade, which was making its way south from the Graveyard Road to Ransom's right. But Smith would not arrive until around 2 P.M.[17]

While McPherson's right was silent, in his center, John A. Logan attacked as scheduled. The 3rd Louisiana Redan was assigned to John E. Smith's brigade, while John D. Stevenson's brigade was ordered to attack the Great Redoubt, 330 yards southwest of the 3rd Louisiana Redan. Mortimer D. Leggett's brigade was held in reserve. Just after 10 A.M., John E. Smith's attacking column, which had been hidden in a deep ravine east of the white Shirley House on the Jackson Road, suddenly emerged from the ground like a swarm of yellow jackets. With the 23rd Indiana in the lead, the columns of fours double-timed down the dusty Jackson Road toward the redan, just over four hundred yards away. The Hoosiers were closely followed by the 20th Illinois. When the vanguard reached a point 140 yards east of the redan, where the road cut its way through a knoll, a hail of lead and iron slapped into the men. The 23rd veered right onto a spur north of the road to seek cover, only to be raked by fire from the 38th Mississippi in the rifle pits north of the redan. The 20th Illinois, however, continued undaunted through the road cut. As soon as the head of the regiment emerged from the meager cover of the cut the murderous fire from the redan chewed through the Illini and forced the regiment to veer to the left, where the bewildered men sought the cover of the south face of the fort. Ira Blanchard of the 20th recalled that the men "could go no farther as the side was almost perpendicular." General Smith, seeing the travails of both regiments, called off the attack and ordered the 23rd Indiana to withdraw from the spur. The hapless men of the 20th Illinois hugged the walls of the fort, and had no choice but to wait until dark to exfiltrate from their precarious position.[18]

South of the Jackson Road, General Stevenson took advantage of the terrain and slipped his brigade down a draw and into a ravine five hundred yards due south of the 3rd Louisiana Redan. He then crept his five regiments ninety yards west to the protection of a steep, thirty-foot-high shelf, only three hundred yards from the Great Redoubt. Stevenson described what happened next:

> Having been furnished with scaling ladders, I [divided] my command into two separate columns, the left column consisting of the Eighth Illinois and Thirty-second Ohio Regiments, and the right column consisting of the Seventh Missouri and Eighty-first Illinois, the Seventeenth Illinois . . . being deployed [as skirmishers] on the crest of the hill, as near the works as possible, to cover the advancing columns, the scaling ladders being distributed between the two columns.[19]

The Great Redoubt, manned by soldiers of the 21st and 22nd Louisiana, loomed 127 feet above Stevenson's five regiments, and the ascent to the objective was over three hundred yards of open ground. Per the plan, at 10

A.M. the two columns moved forward. On the right, the Irishmen of the 7th Missouri entered a deep, canyon-like draw, at the end of which was a steep gradient of almost one hundred feet in as many yards to reach the ditch of the redoubt. But in the hollow these panting men, lugging their ladders, were blessed by some protection from the flanking fire from their right, which spewed from the 3rd Louisiana Redan, and from the frontal fire of the Great Redoubt. Then, as the regiment clambered up the slope, it suffered heavy losses when the exhausted soldiers reached the ditch of the redoubt and received point-blank fire. To add to their woes, the sweating soldiers discovered that their ladders were too short to span the fort's ditch. To the left of the Irishmen the 81st Illinois followed a draw upward to a point 130 yards from the fort. As the men debouched from the draw, they were ordered into line formation, where they became the victims of frontal and enfilading fire from the Confederates of Louis Hébert's brigade. To counter the flanking fire from the 7th Mississippi Battalion and the 36th Mississippi to the left of the Illini, Stevenson ordered the 8th Illinois, his left flank regiment, to lie down and provide covering fire for the men of the 81st. Further to the right, the 32nd Ohio followed suit and took cover behind a ledge 170 yards from the Great Redoubt to provide covering fire for the men of the 7th Missouri. The shower of lead from the Confederate lines proved to be too much, and when the tempestuous but popular regimental commander of the 81st Illinois, James J. Dollins, was killed, Stevenson realized the futility of the attack and withdrew his regiments.[20]

Why did Stevenson's brigade receive fire on its flanks, which stalled the 8th Illinois and 32nd Ohio, or 50 percent of the brigade, and helped kill or wound 98 men of the 81st Illinois and 102 men of the 7th Missouri? J. E. Smith's weak attack on the 3rd Louisiana Redan on the Jackson Road explains the flanking fire on Stevenson's right. But the area on Stevenson's left was assigned to Quinby's Seventeenth Corps division, with Boomer's brigade forming the division right and Sanborn's brigade the division left, while Holmes's brigade was held in reserve. The division was formed in the same ravine used by Stevenson's brigade but was four hundred yards east of its objective due to the southwest angle of the Confederate line. Sanborn wrote that he and Boomer spent the night of May 21 "reconnoitering for the best approaches for infantry to the enemy's works in our front."[21]

Early on the morning of May 22, the two colonels advanced their brigades 130 yards, to a ridge three hundred yards from Hébert's and John C. Moore's Confederate brigades. As the Federals crested the ridge they came under intense artillery and small arms fire. James C. Mahan of the 59th Indiana in Sanborn's brigade recalled that, "we were only a few hundred yards from the rebel forts, but they had discovered our movement and opened fire on us. We dropped to the ground behind the crest of a ridge, and, for the next three hours, could neither advance nor retreat, without danger of being annihilated." To reach the defenses the Federals would have to cross a sixty-foot deep, abatis-choked ravine, and Sanborn wrote:

> Colonel Boomer had some doubts as to his ability to carry the works in his front, and as the works left in my front could not be held, if carried, while those on the right were in possession of the enemy, I transferred to him, for the purpose of this assault, the Fifty-Ninth Indiana Regiment, and deployed the Eighteenth Wisconsin along our whole front as skirmishers. These dispositions being made, the commanders of regiments were ordered to advance upon the works immediately upon the movement commencing on our right. For some reason the troops on our right did not move, and I retained the same position with some loss till about 3 o'clock, when I received an order from General McPherson, through General Quinby, commanding division, to move at once and vigorously upon the works. A staff officer was dispatched immediately to the regimental commanders to communicate this order, but before he had succeeded in doing to it was countermanded.[22]

John E. Tourtellotte, commander of the 4th Minnesota in Sanborn's brigade on the left, reported that his regiment was "ordered to charge upon one of the enemy's forts just in front as soon as I should see a charge made upon the fort next on my right. All preparations were made, and we were waiting for the signal to advance, when I was directed not to advance until further orders." On the right of Boomer's brigade, Ezekiel S. Sampson, commander of the 5th Iowa, reported that his regiment "advanced to the range of hills nearest to the enemy's works, on the left of the large fort commanding the entrance to Vicksburg [Great Redoubt] . . . where we were formed in line of battle, my regiment occupying the right of the front line. . . . Here we remained, beneath a burning sun, and exposed in a measure to the fire on the enemy, until 3 P.M." Another member of the 5th Iowa, John Quincy Adams Campbell, provided more detail:

> This morning at 7 o'clock our brigade was moved forward over a ridge, in our advance to a ravine within 400 yards of the rebels works. We were there drawn up in line and ordered to "rest." Thus far we knew nothing of the *meaning* [Campbell's emphasis] of our move but the riddle was soon solved by Stevenson's brigade of Logan's division coming up and passing us with twenty or thirty *ladders*. There was

no mistaking this sign—the rebel works were to be *stormed*. We soon moved to a position at the brow of the ridge in our front. . . . Most of our brigade, however, was unable to fire from the position we were in. . . . We were compelled to lie flat on the ground for protection and the heat was so great that our suffering became almost intolerable. . . . Stevenson's brigade moved steadily on till they reached the rebel works when they found their ladders were too short and after standing awhile under a withering fire, they were ordered back. . . . I have learned since the charge that our brigade was ordered to follow Stevenson's but (fortunately for us) Col. Boomer did not understand the orders he received. After remaining in our position for several hours . . . we were ordered down off the hill and marched to the rear.[23]

The question has to be asked: Why did Boomer's brigade, which was to initiate the right-to-left en echelon attack for Quinby's division, not advance? Colonel Boomer was killed late on the afternoon of May 22, so his reasoning went to the grave with him. His successor, Holden Putnam, cryptically reported:

On the 22d, a charge was ordered by the whole line at 10 o'clock. This brigade moved forward about a quarter of a mile at 8 A.M., formed in the hollow, slightly protected from the fire of the enemy, each regiment in column, closed by division, the 93rd Illinois on the right, 10th Iowa next, 26th Missouri next, and the 5th Iowa on the left. At 10 o'clock we pushed forward to the crest of the next hill, but were met by a terrible storm of grape, canister, and musketry, and the ground being almost impassable from gullies, covered by a heavy *abatis* of fallen trees, underbrush, vines, etc., the whole position enfiladed by the guns of the enemy, the brigade commander ordered a halt for a few moments.

It is understandable that the situation could have caused Boomer to halt his brigade until he could sort things out, but "a few moments," according to Putnam, was actually almost five hours. Did Boomer "not understand the orders" as Campbell believed, or was there another reason? Perhaps the answer lies in the convolutions of the terrain. Harvey M. Trimble, adjutant of the 93rd Illinois in Boomer's brigade provided a valuable clue:

At 10 o'clock A.M., the regiment took an advanced position on the left of Fort Hill [Federal name for 3rd Louisiana Redan]. The brigade had orders to . . . remain there until the brigade [Stevenson's] next on its right, of General Logan's division, should advance. Then the whole line was to have moved on the enemy's works. . . . The brigade on the right did not move, and consequently this command advanced no farther.

Trimble, of course, is incorrect; Stevenson's brigade did advance. But was Boomer unaware that Stevenson had attacked? When Boomer ordered his brigade to halt on the ridge less than three hundred yards from the Confederate line, and the Confederates to Boomer's front shifted fire to the left into Stevenson's brigade, Stevenson had the 8th Illinois go to ground to provide suppressing fire. But the 8th Illinois was on the south side of a rise, while the remainder of Stevenson's brigade was north of the rise and out of Boomer's sight. So due to the terrain, Boomer, like adjutant Trimble, may not have realized that Stevenson was attacking when he saw the 8th Illinois go to ground. Boomer may have assumed that the other regiments of Stevenson's brigade had done the same. The volume of fire, smoke, and dust could have left Boomer in the Clausewitzian fog of war. Of course, what was in Boomer's mind has been forever lost, but even if this was the reason that he did not attack, his brigade was in Quinby's division, not Logan's, and his orders to attack were not predicated on Stevenson's attack. In any case, the butterfly effect was that when Boomer did not attack, Sanborn, whose attack was predicated on Boomer's, remained in place. Consequently, the men on both flanks of Quinby's division paid the price, evidenced by the Federal casualty rate in front of the Great Redoubt: Boomer's brigade suffered 19 killed and wounded, while Stevenson's brigade lost 272.[24]

The responsibility for the failure of Boomer's brigade to attack reaches higher. Why did not division commander Quinby, corps commander McPherson, or army commander Grant correct the problem? Little is known of Quinby's actions that morning, and it is possible that he was sick in bed. During the Yazoo Pass Expedition in March he had developed an illness that "rendered a change of climate" and he had been given twenty days leave to recuperate. He stated in his report, which, incidentally, concluded two days *before* the assault:

> I was unable to rejoin my command until the morning of the 16th [of May] just as it was about to perform its part in the battle of Champion's Hill. It was deemed inexpedient to relieve Brigadier-General [Marcellus M.] Crocker then commanding, and assign me to the command of the division at the moment it was engaging the enemy. Besides, my still feeble condition, and the exhaustion consequent upon a ride of 16 miles before the ground was gained, incapacitated me for the command. I remained on the field, however, until the battle was ours.

After the failed attack of May 22, Quinby was again sent to the North on sick leave on June 3. He boarded a steamboat to go upriver en route to his home in upstate New York, and finally resigned his commission on December 31, 1863. Quinby never filed a report for May 22, 1863, and his actions on that day remain a mystery. Interestingly, Quinby ranked sixth in Grant's U.S. Military Academy class of 1843, and at West Point Quinby became a lifelong friend of Grant. During Grant's two terms as president he appointed Quinby as United States marshal for the northern district of New York from 1869 to 1877. As to McPherson, like Quinby, he never filed a report of his actions on May 22. His report of the Vicksburg Campaign ends on May 19, when the army arrived before Vicksburg. Of course, McPherson was killed fourteen months later on July 22, 1864, at Atlanta. McPherson, too, was a favorite of Grant, and the young officer's meteoric rise from first lieutenant to major general in less than fifteen months was due to Grant. Finally, there was Grant, who during the attack was with McPherson less than one thousand yards northeast of Quinby's division. Yet Grant never mentioned the failure of Quinby's division to press the fight on the morning of May 22. In the final analysis, regardless of the reason for the inaction of Quinby's division, five thousand men did not participate in the morning attack, allowing the Confederates to shift both fire and reserves to threatened points. Moreover, while McPherson's effort was certainly better than Sherman's, the young general went at the task half-heartedly. Skirmishers aside, out of the twelve thousand soldiers in the Seventeenth Corps, McPherson managed to commit a meager one-tenth of them in the four regiments that assaulted the 3rd Louisiana Redan and the Great Redoubt.[25]

Unlike what was done on the Union right and center, the attack on the left was planned feverishly by McClernand. He established a fire support plan by placing Alvin P. Hovey in charge of twenty-two of the forty-five guns of the Thirteenth Corps. Hovey was a man who loved his artillery, and at the Battles of Port Gibson and Champion Hill he had proven his knowledge of massing fires. He was described as "somewhat eccentric" in that "he believed he was a reincarnation of Napoléon Bonaparte, and that he used to retire to solitary contemplation on the anniversary of the death of the great Corsican." Of course, Napoléon loved his artillery and used it effectively, so McClernand made good use of Hovey's peculiar trait. After placing Hovey on the left with four batteries, McClernand positioned himself in the center of his corps at Battery Maloney, atop a knoll six hundred yards east of the Railroad Redoubt and immediately south of the railroad. Here he was positioned with two twenty-pounder Parrott rifles of the 7th Michigan Battery and two thirty-pounder Parrotts of the Regular Army's 1st U.S. Infantry. Added punch was provided by a third thirty-pounder Parrott manned by the

1st Infantry Regulars, positioned forty yards north of Battery Maloney on the north side of the railroad. All of McClernand's guns opened at daybreak, and by 10 A.M. the well-coordinated and concentrated fire had punched holes in several places, including a huge breach at the salient angle of the Railroad Redoubt. McClernand's guns had also permanently silenced three guns in the Railroad Redoubt and one in the 2nd Texas Lunette.[26]

For the attack, McClernand assigned two brigadier generals to serve as the left and right wing commanders. Eugene A. Carr, who graduated from West Point in 1850, was given four brigades and directed to make the main attack on the 2nd Texas Lunette and the Railroad Redoubt on the right, while Peter J. Osterhaus was to conduct a three-brigade diversion on the Square Fort on the left. McClernand also had to be concerned about a huge two-and-one-half-mile gap between his left flank and the Confederate South Fort adjacent to the Mississippi River. This line was manned by the Confederates and could not be ignored, so McClernand sent the 2nd Illinois Cavalry out to his left to cover the area and build campfires along the line to deceive the Confederates. Grant, too, was aware of this gap, and he advised McArthur, one of McPherson's division commanders who was south of Vicksburg with Hall's brigade, of the planned attack and ordered him to "move with your entire force on the Vicksburg [Warrenton] road, toward the city." The night before the attack, Hall's brigade was encamped at Hennessey's Bayou on the Warrenton Road, two and one-half miles south of the South Fort.[27]

On McClernand's right, Carr assigned two brigades for the assault on the 2nd Texas Lunette, William P. Benton's and Stephen G. Burbridge's, and two brigades to attack the Railroad Redoubt, Michael K. Lawler's and William J. Landrum's. Benton's men, some with scaling ladders, formed in a narrow ravine to the right of the Baldwin's Ferry Road. They approached in column, with the 99th Illinois in the lead, followed by the 33rd Illinois, the 8th Indiana, and the 18th Indiana. Bayonets were fixed, and to ensure that Grant's order was strictly obeyed, the rifle-muskets were not loaded. When the cannon fell silent at 10 A.M. the column moved up the ravine, company by company, and when about halfway up the ravine, on the command, "On left into line," one by one the companies of the first three regiments formed their battle lines. The regimental historian of the 33rd Illinois described the action:

> As soon as the first company of the leading regiment came out of the head of the ravine, the concentrated fire from the fort and a long series of trenches and rifle pits burst upon it and tore it to pieces. The same fate came upon the other companies in quick succession. The wounded came crawling back upon the 33rd that was winding up

the narrow way. This spectacle, with the awful roar and turmoil just ahead, was a frightful indication of what was in store for us. . . . A rod or two from the head of the ravine there was a wagon road [Baldwin's Ferry Road] leading into Vicksburg; balls and shells were ripping along this road like storm-driven hail, and our way was straight across it.[28]

A Texan recalled that Benton's men came at them yelling, "Vicksburg or hell!" Benton's men received the latter when the twelve-pounder gun in the lunette belched canister into the ranks of blue. Coupled with the small arms fire, the barrier of iron and lead forced Benton's first three regiments to veer to the left after crossing the road, where they angled southwest of the lunette toward the rifle pits manned by the 42nd Alabama and the two right companies of the 2nd Texas. Benton's trailing regiment, the 18th Indiana, remained in column formation and, rather than veer left, continued forward into the ditch of the lunette. The unit history states, "Fifty men on the right of the regiment rushed into the deep, wide ditch, while the remainder crowded up to its edge, Sergt. Francis M. Foss planting the colors there."[29]

Burbridge's brigade soon followed Benton's men into the ravine. Burbridge's four regiments surged straight up the hollow and, debouching onto the road, formed a battle line with the 16th Indiana on the left, the 83rd Ohio in the center, the 67th Indiana on the right, and the 23rd Wisconsin in reserve. The brigade quickly lunged forward into the lunette's ditch, with the left of the 16th Indiana resting on the right of Benton's 18th Indiana, while the men of the 67th Indiana moved to the right and occupied a commanding knoll about ninety yards northeast of the lunette. From the knoll, the 67th poured a blaze of lead into the fort's bewildered defenders. Burbridge wrote in his report, "By 10:30 A.M. we had silenced their batteries to a great extent, and the regiments had their colors flying against the walls of the fort. There being some symptoms of an attempt to turn our flanks, I sent four companies of the Twenty-third Wisconsin to support the Sixty-seventh Indiana on the right." Since Quinby's division on Burbridge's right had not attacked, Burbridge was correct in the assumption that his right flank was in the air—the same situation that A. J. Smith had experienced on May 20.[30]

The time to force a conclusion had arrived, and Burbridge committed the rest of his reserve by sending the six remaining companies of the 23rd Wisconsin into the ditch to support the 18th Indiana. The men in the ditch then attempted to storm the lunette by scaling the parapet while firing into the embrasure. The Mississippi artillerymen in the fort attempted to return fire through the embrasure with their twelve-pounder and were mercilessly shot down. Soon the lunette was filled with suffocating smoke, the result of bags of cotton, used as a traverse in the lunette, being set afire by the point-blank rifle blasts. The acrid smoke choked and blinded the soldiers, and it looked as though the 2nd Texas Lunette would fall.[31]

Meanwhile, just over four hundred yards south of the 2nd Texas Lunette, the assault on the Railroad Redoubt raged. Lawler's brigade, consisting of the 21st and 22nd Iowa and the 11th Wisconsin, was the tip of the spear, with Landrum's brigade in support. Since Lawler had only three regiments and Landrum had five, Landrum's 97th Illinois was temporarily attached to Lawler. Ten hours before the scheduled hour of the attack, the aggressive Lawler had "moved over the hill in front of Maloney's siege battery that night." An officer in the 22nd Iowa recalled, "About 12 or 1 midnight, we were quickly awakened, and formed into line and marched quietly down the side of the ridge, across the ravine and immediately under the fort, about 50 yards from the main structure, Fort Beauregard [Railroad Redoubt]. . . . The bugs and beetles, only, are allowed to make a noise."[32]

Lawler formed his regiments in line of battle with the 22nd Iowa on the right, supported by the 21st Iowa, and the 11th Wisconsin on the left, supported by the 97th Illinois. To support Lawler's attack, Landrum's brigade was formed behind a ridge 360 yards east of the Railroad Redoubt, in double column of attack with the 77th Illinois and the 48th Ohio on the right and the 19th Kentucky and 130th Illinois on the left. When the cannonade ceased at 10 A.M., Lawler's battle line, with bayonets fixed, surged forward through the smoke and dust. The 22nd Iowa charged straight up the steep hill to the Railroad Redoubt, and the 11th Wisconsin, due to the terrific fire, veered into the hollow on the left of the fort. The 21st Iowa and the 97th Illinois were dutifully on the heels of the leading regiments. Once at the redoubt, the 22nd Iowa, followed by the 21st Iowa, muscled their way into the ditch of the redoubt, where the vanguard entered a gaping hole that had been blown in the rampart by the artillery barrage. Two daring sergeants, Joseph E. Griffith and Nicholas C. Messenger, entered the fort with a dozen Iowans, forcing a detachment of the 30th Alabama, which manned the cramped interior of the fort, to evacuate the bastion. The Iowans hunkered down in the fort, and according to Colonel William M. Stone, commanding the 22nd Iowa, it was barely 10:10 A.M., and his men "held it . . . for over an hour." Stone also reported that the Confederates "retired from the pits between the two forts, and went down the hill into the ravine or hollow beyond toward the city, leaving only a few straggling sharpshooters behind."[33]

To support Lawler's brigade, Landrum's brigade emerged from behind the protective ridge and traversed the crest, where they "encountered a terrible fire of shell and shot." Yet they descended into the ravine and up the steep hillside to the ditch of the Railroad Redoubt, where Stone ordered the color sergeant of the 77th Illinois to plant his colors, as the colors of the 22nd Iowa were "down in the hollow on the left." Stone quickly had his colors brought forward, and soon the colors of the 22nd Iowa, the 77th Illinois, the 48th Ohio, and 130th Illinois were flying on the rampart. An elated Colonel Stone met with Colonel Cornelius Dunlap of the 21st Iowa "on the highest and most exposed point near the fort," where the two commanders congratulated each other and pondered their next move. Stone said that he "sent word back to General Carr to send me a brigade and I would hold the works," and that he "regarded the door to Vicksburg as opened." Stone later lamented, "Had we been re-enforced at any time before 12 m. by a fresh brigade, I have no doubt that the whole army could have gone into Vicksburg." As Stone and Dunlap spoke on the parapet, musketry rang out from the "woods behind the rifle pits." Dunlap was killed by a bullet to the brain, and Stone received a wound in the arm. The Federals had stepped into a bed of fire ants, and the Confederates were swarming to drive out the intruders. Seeing this, Lawler sent a courier to McClernand requesting reinforcements, and ordered his men to stand fast and hold onto their hard-earned gains.[34]

On McClernand's left, Osterhaus marshaled two of his three brigades in a ravine 470 yards south of the Railroad Redoubt. In the hollow, his men were in supporting distance of Carr's attack, and the site provided some cover. Additionally, three spurs reached out from the Confederate ridgeline to form two ravines, which promised some protection during the approach. William T. Spicely's brigade was Osterhaus's reserve force, and was positioned on the far left to protect that open flank.[35]

Osterhaus attacked with three columns, Daniel W. Lindsey commanded the right and center columns, and James Keigwin commanded the left. Lindsey's two columns entered the two ravines to the right and center, while Keigwin veered left and crossed a bare ridge three hundred yards northeast of the Square Fort. The two right columns entered the abatis and crossed the bottom of a ravine to within two hundred yards of the rifle pits, only to be stopped by Confederate fire. The left column crossed the ridge top three hundred yards northeast of the Square Fort, where the lead regiment, the 7th Kentucky, received galling fire from the 20th Alabama in the fort. Osterhaus's attack ended in a matter of minutes, and since there had been no breakthrough and no threat on the Union left, Spicely's brigade remained unengaged.[36]

McClernand, from his position at Battery Maloney, was six hundred yards from both the 2nd Texas Lunette and the Railroad Redoubt. He could clearly see his flags flying on the two bastions. He could see that the Railroad Redoubt had been breached, and he understood that the window of opportunity was open. Looking seven hundred yards to his left in Osterhaus's front, he saw little progress, so he sent a message to Osterhaus: "General: You must advance and assault the enemy, and thereby make a diversion. If you can't do so, let me know it. In that case you can stand on the defensive, and I will apply General Hovey's [now Spicely's] brigade—at least a part—in support of Carr. One or other of these things must be done." McClernand wanted Spicely's brigade to exploit the breakthrough at the Railroad Redoubt, but it was not sent for never-explained reasons. Possibly Osterhaus did not release it because it was on McClernand's uncovered left flank, but the brigade remained unengaged. So McClernand signaled a message at 11:15 A.M. to Grant, who was one and one-half miles north at Mt. Ararat, saying, "I am hotly engaged. The enemy are pressing me on the right and left. If McPherson would attack, it would make a diversion."[37]

McClernand could see that the Confederate reserves were responding quickly to the crises at the 2nd Texas Lunette and Railroad Redoubt. Since Quinby's division was not applying pressure on McClernand's right, the Confederate reserves in that sector were swarming to the two forts. Martin E. Green's reserve brigade, stationed less than one-half mile behind Moore's lines near the supply depot on Stout's Bayou in the Confederate center, moved to reinforce Moore at noon but was diverted to the Railroad Redoubt due to the Union breakthrough. Upon arriving at the redoubt Green found that another reserve force, Thomas N. Waul's Texas Legion, had already arrived. Green quickly shifted his troops to the beleaguered 2nd Texas Lunette. McClernand was fighting two battles—his and McPherson's.[38]

Grant could easily have turned to McPherson and ordered him to get Quinby's division moving. After all, Quinby was only one-half mile southeast of McPherson and Grant. Instead, in a repeat performance of May 20, Grant patronized McClernand. His reply was signaled from Mt. Ararat at 11:50 A.M., while the Railroad Redoubt was still occupied by Stone's Federals and while possession of the 2nd Texas Lunette was under contention. Grant's reply read, "If your advance is weak, strengthen it by drawing from your reserve or other parts of the lines." Amazingly, while the window of opportunity was open, Grant frittered away critical moments with patronizing advice. Meanwhile, Pemberton made the best of Grant's mistake by committing his reserves wisely.[39]

McClernand received Grant's "draw from your reserve" dispatch before noon and quickly signaled to Grant, "We have gained the enemy's intrenchments at several points, but are brought to a stand. I have sent word to McArthur to re-enforce me if he can. Would it not be best to concentrate the whole or part of his command at this point? P.S. I have received your dispatch. My troops are all engaged, and I cannot withdraw any to re-enforce others." Then, at noon, a harried McClernand hurried off another message—a note that was destined to be embroiled in controversy, "We are hotly engaged with the enemy. We have part possession of two forts, and the Stars and Stripes are floating over them. A vigorous push ought to be made all along the line." Before receiving this message, Grant rode north to the Graveyard Road to see Sherman instead of south to see McClernand. If Grant had any doubts as to what to do, and clearly he did, why did he not ride to consult with McClernand and see the situation for himself? Years later Grant stated to reporter John Russell Young, "The only eyes a general can trust are his own." At this critical moment Grant rode in the wrong direction. In his report Grant wrote, "The position [Mt. Ararat] occupied by me during most of the time of the assault gave me a better opportunity of seeing what was going on in front of the Thirteenth Army Corps than I believed it possible for the commander of it to have." Yet Grant's position at Mt. Ararat was just under one and one-half miles from the 2nd Texas Lunette, and almost one and three-quarter miles from the Railroad Redoubt, while McClernand was positioned just over one-third mile from each fort. Distance aside, the smoke and dust of battle would have almost certainly obscured any possible view of McClernand's front from Mt. Ararat. Simply stated, Grant was disingenuous at best and deceitful at worst.[40]

Sherman wrote in his *Memoirs* that after his assault had been beaten back, "General Grant came to where I was, on foot, having left his horse some distance to the rear. I pointed out to him the rebel works, admitted that my assault had failed, and he said the result with McPherson and McClernand was about the same." Sherman recalled that at that moment McClernand's "part possession of two forts" message arrived and Grant read it, then handed it to him. Grant wrote in his report that McClernand stated "positively and unequivocally that he was in possession of and still held two of the enemy's forts; that the American flag then waved over them, and asking me to have Sherman and McPherson make a diversion in his favor." Sherman recalled the message, saying that it "was in General McClernand's handwriting, to the effect that 'his troops had captured the rebel parapet in his front.' That 'the flag of the Union waved over the stronghold of Vicksburg,' and asking him (General Grant) to give renewed orders to McPherson and Sherman to press their attacks on their respective fronts, lest the enemy should concentrate on him (McClernand)." Sherman then wrote that General Grant said, "I don't believe a word of it." While Grant understandably left his disbelief out of his report, his statement of doubt was corroborated. Standing nearby were several officers of Tuttle's reserve division, and Captain James H. Greene of the 8th Wisconsin recalled that Generals Sherman, Tuttle, Joseph A. Mower, and Adjutant General John A. Rawlins were present. Greene wrote that "General Grant had on a slouch hat, a torn blouse, and eye glass slung over his shoulder." He stated that the generals held a conference at the head of his regiment and that he and several of the officers went forward and heard the conversation. Greene wrote:

> Gen. Grant said he had a dispatch from Gen. McClernand . . . stating that his troops had carried the enemy's works, and were now in them, and if another charge were made on another part of the line . . . he could go into the city. I heard Gen. Grant say that he did not think it was true—but it might be so, and in order that the enterprise might not fail for lack of support he would order another charge to be made immediately.

Grant, therefore, questioned the veracity of his senior corps commander, in front of not only another general officer but also numerous others, to include junior officers. Confederate general Richard Taylor described a similar indiscretion on the part of Braxton Bragg by cogently saying, "Such a declaration, privately made, would have been serious; but publicly, and certain to be repeated, it was astonishing."[41]

Sherman recalled that Grant said "he would instantly ride down the line to McClernand's front, and if I did not receive orders to the contrary, by 3 o'clock P.M., I might try it again." However, three hours had passed since McClernand's first message, and the window of opportunity had slammed shut. The Confederate reserves were in the Railroad Redoubt and the 2nd Texas Lunette, and other troops had been shifted to the threatened points. All that followed was a useless expenditure of soldiers' lives. Then, contrary to what Sherman said, Grant did not ride to see McClernand. Instead, he returned to Mt. Ararat and sent another message to McClernand: "McArthur advanced from Warrenton last night. He is on your left. Communicate with him, and use his forces to the best advantage." Once again, Grant's message was meaningless, because McArthur was with Hall's brigade on the Warrenton road, almost three miles from McClernand's left flank, and Hall was engaged with the Confederate defenses at that point. Then finally, at 2:30 P.M., Grant sent a message to McClernand to advise that Quinby's division would be sent south to assist the Thirteenth Corps. It was too little, too late.[42]

At 3 P.M., Sherman launched his "diversion." Since Giles Smith's and Ransom's brigades were finally in position opposite Green's Redan, Sherman ordered them forward, and they received a quick and brutal repulse. At 4 P.M., Sherman sent Tuttle's reserve division down the Graveyard Road, with Mower's "Eagle Brigade" in the lead. Just as in the morning attack, the lead regiment, the 11th Missouri, was cut to pieces in the beaten zone at the road cut, as was the 47th Illinois, which followed. Before the 8th Wisconsin, with its famed mascot "Old Abe," the bald eagle, and the 5th Minnesota entered the kill zone, Sherman called off the attack. On the far right at 4 P.M., Steele belatedly attacked with two brigades, John M. Thayer's and Charles R. Wood's, across Mint Spring Bayou toward the 26th Louisiana Redoubt. Again, no breakthrough was made. In the Union center, McPherson's "diversion" was remarkably weak. At 3 P.M., the 45th Illinois was sent charging down the Jackson Road toward the 3rd Louisiana Redan and was cut up so badly that its supporting regiment, the 20th Ohio, did not advance. At 3 P.M. Quinby left Sanborn's 18th Wisconsin in place along the division front, and per Grant's orders, executed a two-mile, circuitous march with his three brigades to the vicinity of Battery Maloney. McClernand sent Boomer's and Sanborn's brigades to Carr, while Holmes's brigade was sent to Osterhaus. Carr then sent Sanborn's three remaining regiments to reinforce Burbridge's brigade at the 2nd Texas Lunette, while Boomer's men were sent to the Railroad Redoubt. Darkness was closing, and while Sanborn moved into position at the lunette, he merely occupied Burbridge's positions. To the south, Osterhaus decided it was too late in the day for an assault, and did not commit Holmes's brigade. But Boomer's brigade advanced toward the rifle pits between the 2nd Texas Lunette and the Railroad Redoubt under a withering fire. Boomer was killed at the head of his men and the attack was over, ending the day's fighting. At day's end on May 22, the butcher's bill for Grant's army was 502 killed, 2,550 wounded, and 147 missing, for a total of 3,199. Confederate reports were not made, but their casualties were probably around 500.[43]

Grant had to be embarrassed for Sherman and McPherson. In the morning attack, Sherman, in the attack on the Stockade Redan, engaged only one of his forty-one regiments available, along with the 150 men of the "Forlorn Hope." McPherson did somewhat better that morning by engaging five of his thirty available regiments: Two attacked the 3rd Louisiana Redan and three attacked the Great Redoubt. McClernand, however, committed twenty-five of his thirty regiments against the 2nd Texas Lunette, the Railroad Redoubt, and the Square Fort. Yet McClernand was blamed for the day's disaster. According to Captain William L. B. Jenney, an engineer officer in Sherman's Fifteenth Corps:

> That night there were stirring times at Grant's headquarters, where most of the corps and division commanders were assembled. Mc-Clernand was spoken of in no complimentary terms. Rawlins ordered Major [Theodore S.] Bower[s] to open the record book and charge a thousand lives to that —— McClernand. Rawlins used strong language when the occasion required, and this was one of them. The only

works McClernand had captured were some advanced picket posts abandoned by the enemy before our line came in sight.

The day had been a disaster for Grant, and it was clear that McClernand, not Sherman, McPherson, or Quinby, was to be the scapegoat. The gossip and slandering in Grant's camp, while unseemly and unprofessional, was a harbinger of actions against McClernand. On May 24, Grant wrote to General in Chief Henry W. Halleck, saying in part, "The assault was made simultaneously by the three army corps at 10 A.M. The loss on our side was not very heavy at first, but . . . General McClernand's dispatches misled me as to the real state of facts, and caused much of this loss." There are no secrets in an army, and McClernand, upon hearing of the accusations against him, wrote to Grant on June 4, complaining of "a systematic effort to destroy my usefulness and character as a commander." But the die was cast and Grant never answered McClernand. After all, someone had to be blamed for 3,199 needless casualties. The acrimony in Grant's camp continued until McClernand was relieved of command on June 18.[44]

Grant's Vicksburg Campaign was brilliant and was certainly his finest, but despite Grant's assertion, even the Vicksburg Campaign could have been improved. Grant knew this, for he wrote in his *Memoirs*, "I always regretted that the last assault at Cold Harbor was ever made. I might say the same thing of the assault of the 22nd of May, 1863, at Vicksburg." But then he dedicated almost two full pages to the justification of the May 22 attack—an almost verbatim repetition of his reasons stated earlier in his work.[45]

Captain Jenney wrote that during the Vicksburg Campaign, "Grant adopted the motto, 'Waste no time in trying to shift the responsibility of failure from one to the other, but take things as you find them and make the best of them.'" Despite his words, Grant never assumed the full responsibility for ordering an attack that cost over three thousand Federal casualties. Instead, McClernand became his scapegoat. Moreover, Grant's failure has been largely unrecognized by historians, and McClernand, the only one of Grant's corps commanders who executed the commander's intent on that fateful day, has continued to be the scapegoat. Remarkably, this misrepresentation of history flies in the face of the dictum taught to all U.S. military officers, "The leader alone is responsible for all that his unit does or fails to do. He cannot delegate this responsibility."[46]

Notes

1. John Russell Young, *Around the World with General Grant*, 2 vols. (New York: American News Company, 1879), 1: 11; ibid., 2: 615; John Russell Young, *Men and Memories*, 2 vols. (New York: F. Tennyson Neely, 1901), 2: 476, 481–82; James H.

Wilson, *Under the Old Flag*, 2 vols. (New York: D. Appleton and Company, 1912), 1: 212; Charles A. Dana, *Recollections of the Civil War* (New York: D. Appleton and Company, 1898), 61; *Japan Mail: A Fortnightly Summary of Intelligence from Japan* 3, no. 15 (September 2, 1879), 461; Jean Edward Smith, *Grant* (New York: Simon and Schuster, 2001), 607–8, 613; Patrick O'Brian, *Master and Commander* (New York: W. W. Norton and Company, 1970), 32–33.

2. Headquarters, Department of the Army, *Field Manual No. 100–5, Operations* (Washington, DC: U.S. Government Printing Office, May 1986), 91.

3. U.S. War Department, *The War of the Rebellion: A Compilation of the Official Records of the Union and Confederate Armies*, 128 vols. (Washington, DC: Government Printing Office, 1880–1901), series 1, vol. 24, pt. 1: 54–55. Hereinafter cited as *OR*. All references are to Series 1 unless otherwise indicated. U. S. Grant, *Personal Memoirs of U. S. Grant*, 2 vols. (New York: Charles L. Webster and Company, 1885), 1: 530–31; ibid., 2: 277–78; Francis Vinton Greene, *The Mississippi* (New York: Charles Scribner's Sons, 1882), 177–78; Kenneth P. Williams, *Lincoln Finds a General*, 4 vols. (New York: MacMillan Company, 1956), 4: 389; Edwin C. Bearss, *The Campaign for Vicksburg*, 3 vols. (Dayton: Morningside House, 1986), 3: 787–88; Allan Nevins, *The War for the Union*, 8 vols. (New York: Charles Scribner's Sons, 1971) 3: 65–66; Charles E. Wilcox, "With Grant at Vicksburg," *Journal of the Illinois State Historical Society* 30 (April 1937–January 1938): 478–79.

4. Sun Tzu, *The Art of War*, translated by Samuel B. Griffith (New York: Oxford University Press, 1963), 65; John A. Barnes, *Ulysses S. Grant on Leadership* (Roseville, CA: Prima, 2001), 220; Young, *Men and Memories*, 2: 478; Karl von Clausewitz, *On War*, translated by O. J. Matthijs Jolles (Washington, DC: Combat Forces Press, 1943), 51–52.

5. William T. Sherman, *Memoirs of General W. T. Sherman*, 2 vols. (New York: Charles L. Webster and Company, 1892), 1: 353; Edwin C. Bearss and J. Parker Hills, *Receding Tide: Vicksburg and Gettysburg* (Washington, DC: National Geographic Society, 2010), 238; Richard L. Kiper, *Major General John Alexander McClernand: Politician in Uniform* (Kent, OH: Kent State University Press, 1999), 253–54.

6. Gideon Welles, *The Civil War Diary of Gideon Welles, Lincoln's Secretary of the Navy*, edited by William E. and Erica L. Gienapp (Urbana: Knox College Lincoln Studies Center and University of Illinois Press, 2014), 74; Dana, *Recollections of the Civil War*, 58; *OR*, vol. 24, pt.3: 332; Tamara A. Smith, "A Matter of Trust: Grant and James B. McPherson," and Terrence J. Winschel, "Fighting Politician: John A. McClernand," in *Grant's Lieutenants*, edited by Steven E. Woodworth (Lawrence, KS: University Press of Kansas, 2001), 135, 148, 152.

7. *OR*, vol. 24, pt. 1: 154; ibid., pt. 2: 33; Thomas B. Marshall, *History of the Eighty-Third Ohio Volunteer Infantry* (Cincinnati: Gibson and Perin Company, 1913), 84; Reuben B. Scott, *The History of the 67th Regiment, Indiana Infantry Volunteers* (Bedford, IN: Herald Book and Job Print, 1892), 36; John A. Bering and Thomas Montgomery, *History of the Forty-Eighth Ohio Vet. Vol. Inf.* (Hillsboro, OH: Highland News Office, 1880), 86–87; Bearss, *Campaign for Vicksburg*, 3: 800–801; Kiper, *McClernand: Politician in Uniform*, 254.

8. *OR*, vol. 24, pt. 3: 331–32; Bearss, *Campaign for Vicksburg*, 3: 800–802.

9. James H. Wilson, "A Staff Officer's Journal of the Vicksburg Campaign, April 30 to July 4, 1863," *Journal of the Military Service Institution of the United States*

43 (1908): 263; Warren E. Grabau, *Ninety-Eight Days: A Geographer's View of the Vicksburg Campaign* (Knoxville: University of Tennessee Press, 2000), 355, 378. Mt. Ararat M. B. Church on Culkin Road sits atop Mt. Ararat today. McPherson's headquarters was 240 yards west of Mt. Ararat, in defilade behind Battery McPherson. John Y. Simon, ed., *The Papers of Ulysses S. Grant*, 31 vols. (Carbondale: Southern Illinois University Press, 1967–2009), 8: 239; Kiper, *McClernand: Politician in Uniform*, 254; Ephraim McD. Anderson, *Memoirs: Historical and Personal; including the Campaigns of the First Missouri Confederate Brigade* (repr., Dayton: Morningside Bookshop, 1988), 331; *OR*, vol. 24, pt. 1: 731–32, 772–73, 776, 784; ibid., pt. 2: 206, 262, 285, 292–93, 407, 709–10; Charles E. Affeld Diary, May 20, 1863, Vicksburg National Military Park Archives, Vicksburg, MS; Bearss, *Campaign for Vicksburg*, 3: 794–95, 798; Sherman, *Memoirs*, 1: 354.

10. Simon, *Papers of Ulysses S. Grant*, 8: 239; Harvey M. Trimble, *History of the Ninety Third Regiment, Illinois Volunteer Infantry* (Chicago: Blakely Printing Company, 1898), 35; Bearss, *Campaign for Vicksburg*, 3: 801.

11. Brooks D. Simpson and Jean V. Berlin, *Sherman's Selected Correspondence of the Civil War* (Chapel Hill: University of North Carolina Press, 1999), 471; Michael B. Ballard, *Vicksburg: The Campaign That Opened the Mississippi* (Chapel Hill: University of North Carolina Press, 2004), 335.

12. Charles A. Dana, *The Life of Ulysses S. Grant* (Springfield, MA: Samuel Bowles and Company, 1868), 129; *OR*, vol. 24, pt.1: 154, 171; ibid., pt. 3: 333–34; Simon, *Papers of Ulysses S. Grant*, 8: 245–46; Grant, *Personal Memoirs*, 1: 531; Bearss, *Campaign for Vicksburg*, 3: 806–7.

13. Smith, *Grant*, 252; Bearss, *Campaign for Vicksburg*, 3: 794–95, 797–800, 823–24; *OR*, vol. 24, pt. 1: 55, 154, 709–10; ibid., pt. 2: 19, 181, 206, 229–30, 240, 262, 285, 292–93, 407; ibid., pt. 3: 334–35; Affeld diary, May 22, 1863; F. Senour, *Major General William T. Sherman and His Campaigns* (Chicago: Henry M. Sherwood, Publisher, 1865), 128; Williams, *Lincoln Finds a General*, 4: 389; Bearss and Hills, *Receding Tide*, 239; Isaac H. Elliott, *History of the Thirty-Third Regiment Illinois Veteran Volunteer Infantry* (Gibson City, IL: Press of the Gibson Courier, 1902), 44; F. H. Mason, *The Forty-Second Ohio Infantry: A History* (Cleveland, OH: Cobb, Andrews, and Company, 1876), 221.

14. Sherman, *Memoirs*, 1: 354; *OR*, vol. 24, pt. 3: 334–35; Bearss, *Campaign for Vicksburg*, 3: 814; Grabau, *Ninety-Eight Days*, 369–70; Ballard, *Campaign That Opened the Mississippi*, 338.

15. *OR*, vol. 24, pt. 1: 756–57; ibid., pt. 2: 257, 273; Sherman, *Memoirs*, 1: 354; Joseph A. Saunier, *A History of the Forty-Seventh Regiment, Ohio Veteran Volunteer Infantry* (Hillsboro, OH: Lyle Printing Company, 1903), 147; Lucien B. Crooker, Henry S. Nourse, John G. Brown, *The Story of the Fifty-Fifth Regiment, Illinois Volunteer Infantry* (Clinton, MA: W. J. Coulter, 1887), 244–47; Affeld Diary, May 22, 1863; Anderson, *First Missouri Confederate Brigade*, 331; Bearss, *Campaign for Vicksburg*, 3: 815–16; Bearss and Hills, *Receding Tide*, 240.

16. *OR*, vol. 24, pt. 1: 760; ibid., pt. 2: 251, 257–58; Wilson, "Staff Officer's Journal," 264; Bearss, *Campaign for Vicksburg*, 3: 815–18; Saunier, *Forty-Seventh Ohio*, 146–50; John S. Kountz, *History of the 37th Regiment, O.V.V.I.* (Toledo, OH: Montgomery and Vrooman Printers, 1889), 21–22; Thomas H. Barton, *Autobiography of Dr. Thomas H. Barton, the Self-Made Physician of Syracuse Ohio, Including a History of the Fourth*

Regiment, West Virginia Volunteer Infantry (Charleston, WV: West Virginia Printing Company, 1890), 153; Grabau, *Ninety-Eight Days*, 372; Ballard, *Campaign That Opened the Mississippi*, 338–39; Sherman, *Memoirs*, 1: 354; Bearss, *Campaign for Vicksburg*, 3: 860; Bearss and Hills, *Receding Tide*, 250.

17. *OR*, vol. 24, pt. 2: 287, 300; Joseph Stockton, *War Diary* (Chicago: John T. Stockton, 1910), 16.

18. *OR*, vol. 24, pt. 1: 710, 719; Osborn H. Oldroyd, *A Soldier's Story of the Siege of Vicksburg from the Diary of Osborn H. Oldroyd* (Springfield, IL: Published for the author, 1885), 31–32; Lydia Minturn Post, *Soldiers' Letters from Camp, Battle-Field, and Prison* (New York: Bunce and Huntington, Publishers, 1865), 268; W. H. Tunnard, *A Southern Record: The History of the Third Regiment Louisiana Infantry* (Baton Rouge: Printed for the author, 1866), 239; George H. Woodruff, *Fifteen Years Ago: or the Patriotism of Will County* (Joliet, IL: Joliet Republican Book and Job Steam Printing House, 1876), 126; Ira Blanchard, *I Marched with Sherman: Civil War Memoirs of the 20th Illinois Volunteer Infantry* (San Francisco: J. D. Huff and Company, 1992), 95–96; Bearss, *Campaign for Vicksburg*, 3: 819–20.

19. *OR*, vol. 24, pt. 1: 719; Seth J. Wells, *The Siege of Vicksburg from the Diary of Seth J. Wells* (Detroit: William H. Rowe, Publisher, 1915), 67–68; Bearss, *Campaign for Vicksburg*, 3: 820–22.

20. *OR*, vol. 24, pt. 1: 719; Edmund Newsom, *Experience in the War of the Great Rebellion* (repr., Murphysboro, IL: Jackson County Historical Society, 1984), 50–51; Oldroyd, *Soldier's Story*, 32; Wells, *Siege of Vicksburg*, 67–68; Bearss, *Campaign for Vicksburg*, 3: 820–22.

21. *OR*, vol. 24, pt. 1: 732; 776; Bearss, Campaign for Vicksburg, 3: 822.

22. *OR*, vol. 24, pt. 1: 732, 772–73, 776, 780; James Curtis Mahan, *Memoirs of James Curtis Mahan* (Lincoln, NE: Franklin Press, 1919), 124; Alonzo L. Brown, *History of the Fourth Regiment of Minnesota Infantry Volunteers during the Great Rebellion, 1861–1865* (St. Paul, MN: Pioneer Press, 1892), 213–14, 220; Bearss, *Campaign for Vicksburg*, 3: 822–23.

23. *OR*, vol. 24, pt. 2: 62, 316; Bearss, *Campaign for Vicksburg*, 3: 822–23; Bearss and Hills, *Receding Tide*, 242; John Quincy Adams Campbell, *The Union Must Stand*, edited by Mark Grimsley and Todd D. Miller (Knoxville: University of Tennessee Press, 2000), 99–101.

24. *OR*, vol. 24, pt. 2: 67. Putnam's "divisions" refer to the four divisions of an infantry regiment in battle formation. His regimental positions are as viewed by a commander facing the brigade from the front, rather than a soldier in ranks facing the enemy, hence Putnam's "left" and "right" are reversed, that is, the 93rd Illinois was on the left and the 5th Iowa was on the right; Trimble, *History of the Ninety-Third Illinois*, 35. Fort Hill, in Union accounts, refers to the 3rd Louisiana Redan. Trimble probably considered both the Great Redoubt and the 3rd Louisiana Redan as "Fort Hill"; Union position tablets, Vicksburg National Military Park: "Boomer's Brigade: Assault, May 22, 1863, First Position," GPS 32 21.218 N, 90 50.801 W, and "Stevenson's Brigade: Assault, May 22, 1863," GPS 32 21.450 N, 90 50.785 W.

25. *OR*, vol. 24, pt. 1: 641; ibid., pt. 2: 59–60; Bearss, *Campaign for Vicksburg*, 3: 833; Bearss and Hills, *Receding Tide*, 52, 242; Ezra J. Warner, *Generals in Blue: Lives of Union Commanders* (Baton Rouge: Louisiana State University Press, 1964), 306–7, 387–88; Association of Graduates, USMA, *1980 Register of Graduates and Former*

Cadets, edited by Michael J. Krisman (Chicago: R. R. Donnelley and Sons Company, 1980), 236, 245; Stewart Sifakis, *Who Was Who in the Civil War* (New York: Facts on File Publications, 1988), 424–25, 526–27; Smith, *Grant's Lieutenants,* 151–53, 164.

26. *OR,* vol. 24, pt. 1: 154; ibid., pt. 2: 240; Bearss, *Campaign for Vicksburg,* 3: 800–801, 823–24; *OR,* vol. 24, pt. 1: 154; ibid., pt. 2: 240; Jacob P. Dunn, *Indiana and Indianans,* 5 vols. (Chicago: American Historical Society, 1919), 1: 482; Bearss and Hills, *Receding Tide,* 106, 242–43.

27. *OR,* vol. 24, pt. 1: 171–72; ibid., pt. 2: 301–2; ibid., pt. 3: 334; Association of Graduates, *USMA 1980 Register,* 242; Kiper, *McClernand: Politician in Uniform,* 258; Bearss, *Campaign for Vicksburg,* 3: 721, 805–6, 814, 823, 827–28; Bearss and Hills, *Receding Tide,* 243; Ballard, *Campaign That Opened the Mississippi,* 340; William W. Belknap and Loren S. Tyler, *History of the Fifteenth Regiment, Iowa Veteran Volunteer Infantry* (Keokuk, IA: R. B. Ogden and Son, 1887), 255–56; Joseph E. Chance, *The Second Texas Infantry from Shiloh to Vicksburg* (Austin, TX: Eakin Press, 1984), 105.

28. *OR,* vol. 24, pt. 2: 140–41; Bearss, *Campaign for Vicksburg,* 3: 824, 827, 829; Bearss and Hills, *Receding Tide,* 243; Henry C. Adams Jr., *Indiana at Vicksburg* (Indianapolis, IN: Wm. B. Burford, Contractor for State Printing and Binding, 1911), 188; Elliott, *History of the Thirty-Third Illinois,* 44.

29. Chance, *Second Texas Infantry,* 105; Bearss, *Campaign for Vicksburg,* 3: 828–29; Adams, *Indiana at Vicksburg,* 189; Wilcox, "With Grant at Vicksburg," 480.

30. *OR,* vol. 24, pt. 1: 598; ibid., pt. 2: 34; Bearss, *Campaign for Vicksburg,* 3: 829–30; Bearss and Hills, *Receding Tide,* 244.

31. Marshall, *History of the Eighty-Third Ohio,* 85–86; Chance, *Second Texas Infantry,* 106; Bearss, *Campaign for Vicksburg,* 3: 830–31; Bearss and Hills, *Receding Tide,* 43–244.

32. *OR,* vol. 24, pt. 1: 178; ibid., pt. 2: 140; Samuel C. Jones, *Reminiscences of the Twenty-Second Iowa Volunteer Infantry* (repr., Iowa City, IA: Press of the Camp Pope Bookshop, 1993), 37–38; Bearss, *Campaign for Vicksburg,* 3: 824; Bearss and Hills, *Receding Tide,* 244.

33. *OR,* vol. 24, 1: 178; ibid., pt. 2: 141; Bearss, *Campaign for Vicksburg,* 3: 824–25; Bearss and Hills, *Receding Tide,* 246.

34. *OR,* vol. 24, pt. 1: 154–55, 178; ibid., pt. 2: 140–41, 238; Bearss, *Campaign for Vicksburg,* 3: 826; Bearss and Hills, *Receding Tide,* 246; William Wiley, *The Civil War Diary of a Common Soldier,* edited by Terrence J. Winschel (Baton Rouge: Louisiana State University Press, 2001), 50–51; Wilcox, "With Grant at Vicksburg," 480–81; Bering and Montgomery, *History of the Forty-Eighth Ohio,* 87; Kiper, *McClernand: Politician in Uniform,* 260. The Iowa Memorial in Vicksburg National Military Park graces the crest of the ridge today.

35. *OR,* vol. 24, pt. 2: 20, 240; Bearss, *Campaign for Vicksburg,* 3: 832; Regimental Association, *History of the Forty-Sixth Regiment Indiana Volunteer Infantry* (Logansport, IN: Press of Wilson, Humphreys and Company, 1888), 64; Mary B. Townsend, *Yankee Warhorse: A Biography of Major General Peter Osterhaus* (Columbia: University of Missouri Press, 2010), 109; Kiper, *McClernand: Politician in Uniform,* 260; Bearss and Hills, *Receding Tide,* 247.

36. *OR,* vol. 24, pt. 2: 20–21; Bearss, *Campaign for Vicksburg,* 3: 833; Townsend, *Yankee Warhorse,* 110; Kiper, *McClernand: Politician in Uniform,* 260; Mason, *Forty-Second Ohio,* 221–25.

37. *OR*, vol. 24, pt. 3: 340; Bearss, *Campaign for Vicksburg*, 3: 833; Townsend, *Yankee Warhorse*, 110; Simon, *Papers of Ulysses S. Grant*, 8: 253; *OR*, vol. 24, pt. 1: 172; Bearss, *Campaign for Vicksburg*, 3: 836; Kiper, *McClernand: Politician in Uniform*, 260; Bearss and Hills, *Receding Tide*, 247.

38. *OR*, vol. 24, pt. 2: 357–58, 420; ibid., pt. 3: 907–8; Bearss, *Campaign for Vicksburg*, 3: 850, 858. The Confederate supply depot was on Stout's Bayou, 850 yards northwest of the 2nd Texas Lunette and 300 yards north of Grove Street.

39. Simon, *Papers of Ulysses S. Grant*, 8: 253; *OR*, vol. 24, pt. 1: 172; Bearss, *Campaign for Vicksburg*, 3: 836; Kiper, *McClernand: Politician in Uniform*, 260; Bearss and Hills, *Receding Tide*, 248.

40. Simon, *Papers of Ulysses S. Grant*, 8: 253; *OR*, vol. 24, pt. 1: 55–56, 172–73; Bearss, *Campaign for Vicksburg*, 3: 836; Kiper, *McClernand: Politician in Uniform*, 261; Bearss and Hills, *Receding Tide*, 248–49; Young, *Around the World with General Grant*, 2: 615.

41. Sherman, *Memoirs*, 1: 354–55; *OR*, vol. 24, pt. 1: 55; James H. Greene, *Letters to My Wife: A Civil War Diary from the Western Front*, edited by Sharon L. D. Kraynek (Apollo, PA: Closson Press, 1995), 67; Richard Taylor, *Destruction and Reconstruction* (New York: D. Appleton and Company, 1879), 100.

42. Sherman, *Memoirs*, 1: 355; *OR*, vol. 24, pt. 1: 173; ibid., pt. 2: 301–2; Belknap and Tyler, *History of the Fifteenth Iowa*, 256; Bearss and Hills, *Receding Tide*, 249.

43. *OR*, vol. 24, pt. 1: 173, 598–99, 617, 710, 720, 722, 732–33, 757, 760, 768, 776–77; ibid., pt. 2: 21, 62, 67, 160–66, 238, 240, 251–52, 258, 273, 297–98, 300, 316, 351, 357–58, 360–61, 389, 415; ibid., pt. 3: 340–43, 370–71; Brown, *Fifty-Fifth Illinois*, 243; Wales W. Wood, *A History of the Ninety-Fifth Regiment Illinois Infantry Volunteers* (Chicago: Tribune Company's Book and Job Printing Office, 1865), 76–78; Cloyd Bryner, *Bugle Echoes: The Story of Illinois 47th* (Springfield, IL: Phillips Brothers, Printers and Binders, 1905), 85–86; David W. Reed, *Campaigns and Battles of the Twelfth Regiment Iowa Veteran Volunteer Infantry* (Evanston, IL: Library of Congress, 1903), 123; Alonzo Abernethy, "Incidents of an Iowa Soldier's Life, or Four Years in Dixie," *Annals of Iowa* 12, no. 6 (October 1920), 415; Scott, *History of the 67th Indiana*, 37–38; Adams, *Indiana at Vicksburg*, 189–90, 203; Bering and Montgomery, *History of the Forty-Eighth Ohio*, 88–90; M. Amelia Stone, ed., *Memoir of George Boardman Boomer* (Boston: Rand and Avery, 1864), 258; Bearss, *Campaign for Vicksburg*, 3: 837–52; Union position tablet, Vicksburg National Military Park: "Sanborn's Brigade: Assault, May 22, 1863, " GPS 32 20.751 N, 90 51.197 W.

44. William L. B. Jenney, "Personal Recollections of Vicksburg," *Military Essays and Recollections: Papers Read before the Commandery of the State of Illinois, Military Order of the Loyal Legion of the United States* (Chicago: Dial Press, 1899), 3: 261–62; Bearss and Hills, *Receding Tide*, 250, 254; *OR*, vol. 24, pt. 1: 37, 164–66.

45. Grant, *Personal Memoirs*, 2: 276–78.

46. Jenney, "Personal Recollections," 258; Headquarters, Department of the Army, *Field Manual No. 101–5: Staff Organization and Operations* (Washington, DC: U.S. Government Printing Office, May 1984), 1–2.

3
—

THE ASSAULT ON THE RAILROAD REDOUBT

Steven E. Woodworth

H aving received Grant's orders for a May 22 assault on the Vicksburg defenses, Major General John A. McClernand planned attacks on all three of the major Confederate fortifications within the sector of his Thirteenth Corps. From north to south these were the 2nd Texas Lunette, guarding the Baldwin's Ferry Road; the Railroad Redoubt, covering the Southern Railroad of Mississippi; and the Square Fort. McClernand expected to make his main effort against the center of these fortifications, the Railroad Redoubt. Since it lay only about four hundred yards south of—and was on a line of sight with—the 2nd Texas Lunette and the two were mutually supporting, he would have to attack both works at the same time.[1]

He need not, however, have made more than a demonstration against the Square Fort, which was not tactically interdependent with the Railroad Redoubt. This realization was significant because of the number of troops McClernand had. His corps was composed of four divisions, each containing two brigades. McClernand would not be using Brigadier General Alvin P. Hovey's division, which had been badly shot up at Champion Hill six days earlier. Grant had then detached the division to guard the army's rear at the bridges of the Big Black River but had relented and allowed McClernand to bring up one of Hovey's two brigades, Brigadier General George McGinnis's, once it became clear that there was no imminent Confederate threat from the rear.[2] With the seven brigades at his disposal, McClernand planned to launch two brigades at each of the three Confederate strong points. That would leave him with only McGinnis's brigade as a reserve to follow up any possible success. Making the operation at the Square Fort into a one-brigade demonstration would have freed another brigade for use as a reserve to exploit the breakthrough he hoped to achieve with his main effort at the Railroad Redoubt.

Another significant decision of McClernand's concerned the arrangement of units and command for the attacks on the 2nd Texas Lunette and the

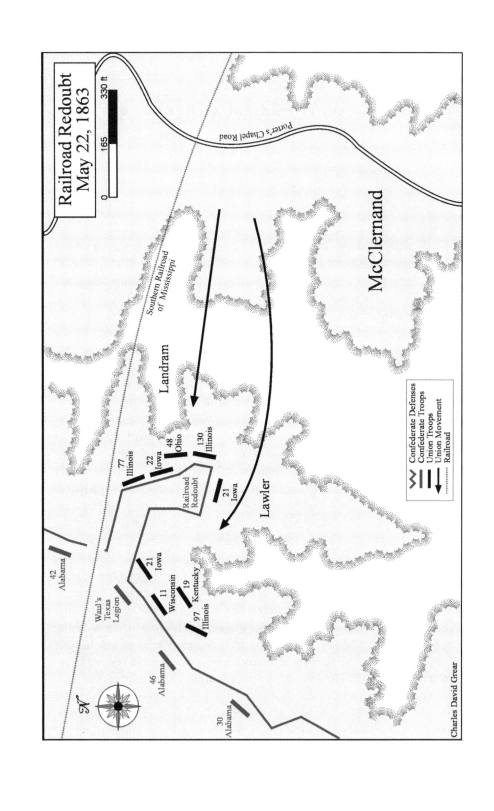

Railroad Redoubt
May 22, 1863

0   165   330 ft

Porter's Chapel Road

McClernand

Southern Railroad
of Mississippi

Landram

77 Illinois

22 Iowa

48 Ohio

130 Illinois

Railroad Redoubt

21 Iowa

Lawler

42 Alabama

Waul's Texas Legion

21 Iowa

11 Wisconsin

19 Kentucky

97 Illinois

46 Alabama

30 Alabama

N

Confederate Defenses
Confederate Troops
Union Troops
Union Movement
Railroad

Charles David Grear

Railroad Redoubt. Since each was to be attacked by two brigades, it would have made sense to assign each as the target of a single two-brigade division, and since the dual assaults were to be the centerpiece of his corps' effort that day, he could have coordinated their advances personally from a command post opposite the two objectives. Instead, he assigned that task to Brigadier General Eugene Carr, who was to use his own division as well as that of A. J. Smith. For some reason, perhaps to maintain his own direct control of the attacks on both objectives, Carr decided to array his own two brigades in the first line, and Smith's two as a second line of battle behind them.[3] Thus the assault on the Railroad Redoubt was to be carried out by Brigadier General Michael K. Lawler's brigade of Carr's division, followed up by Colonel William J. Landram's brigade of Smith's division—with a decidedly murky command structure.

Lawler, whose brigade was to spearhead the main effort at the Railroad Redoubt, noted in his report that he did not receive his orders for the attack until early on the evening of May 21. For the previous twenty-four hours, Lawler's brigade had been on the front lines just south of where the Southern Railroad passed through the line of Confederate fortifications about a mile and three-quarters southeast of the Warren County Courthouse in the center of Vicksburg.[4]

Lawler's brigade had enjoyed spectacular success five days earlier at Big Black River Bridge. There Lawler had sheltered his troops in a meander scar of the river before leading them in a successful charge against the Confederate breastworks. After one deadly volley, the Rebel line had collapsed in the face of the attack, and the brigade rounded up 1,120 prisoners—more men than it had carried into the battle.[5] Casualties were nevertheless significant: 27 dead, 194 wounded, most of them in the hard-hit 23rd Iowa, which had led the attack. That regiment lost its colonel, William H. Kinsman.[6] The 23rd was detailed to guard prisoners after Big Black River Bridge and did not rejoin the brigade during the campaign.[7] The losses had not been in vain, though, as Lawler's charge broke the Confederate line and started a general rout that brought quick and decisive Union victory. Lawler hoped for a similar success in the May 22 attack.[8]

The Confederate works in front of the brigade at Vicksburg were formidable. The key to the sector was a stout earthwork known as the Railroad Redoubt, which besides its infantry defenders also boasted one six-pounder gun and two twelve-pounder howitzers.[9] With walls fifteen feet high, and a ten-foot-wide ditch surrounding it, the redoubt perched on a hilltop thirty feet above the tracks of the Southern Railroad and, at its nearest point, about thirty-five yards to the south of the rails—that is, to the left as viewed from

Union lines. The redoubt protruded forward about two hundred yards from the line of the Rebel rifle pit that ran along its rear face. Thus Confederates in the redoubt could pour an enfilading fire into any Union troops approaching the rifle pit, and the troops in the rifle pit could similarly enfilade any Federals attacking the south face of the redoubt. The position of Lawler's brigade was about four hundred yards from the Railroad Redoubt in a direction more or less parallel to the tracks, which were on the right of Lawler's brigade. The Union line occupied a ridge of almost equal height with the ground on which the redoubt stood, but between the lines the ground fell away sharply into a seventy-foot-deep ravine.[10]

The orders Lawler received on the evening of May 21 presumably stemmed from Carr's headquarters, though Lawler did not name their origin in his report. They specified that the troops were to advance precisely at 10 A.M. the next day, but they apparently indicated that Lawler's effort was to be aimed not expressly at the Railroad Redoubt but merely at the Confederate positions opposite his own. It was probably natural for Carr, as a professionally trained officer, to assume that no commander would contemplate attacking any other point within the sector.

At any rate, Lawler conveyed the order to Colonel William M. Stone of the 22nd Iowa and told the colonel he wanted the 22nd to lead the next morning's assault. He gave Stone substantial tactical control of the brigade's attack, allowing him to choose whatever point he wished on the Confederate line in this sector as the target of his attack. The rest of the brigade would support him.[11]

Stone had to move quickly if he was going to study the Confederate position and its approaches—specifically with an eye to planning an assault—before complete darkness fell. The sun was even then setting or had just set. Through the dusk Stone crept forward, carefully keeping under cover, until he was only fifty yards from the Railroad Redoubt.[12] This feat was possible in part because of the uneven nature of the ground between the opposing lines. The deep ravine between the Union position and the Railroad Redoubt would at first glance seem to be an obstacle to the attackers, but Stone recognized it as in fact the best hope his men had in the coming assault.[13]

The ravine's slopes were too steep to allow the defenders above it, in the redoubt, to deliver fire to the slope nearest their position. Indeed, even the flat ground at the bottom of the ravine would be safe from Confederate fire. That would allow the attackers to use the ravine in the same way the brigade had used the meander scar at Big Black River Bridge. The declivity would serve as a protected place in which to marshal troops in preparation for a final, relatively short rush toward the enemy's line. In his report Stone later wrote, "My observations satisfied me that the fort next to the railroad could be carried more easily and with less sacrifice than any other point on our front, and I determined to direct my regiment against it."[14]

Under the cover of darkness around four o'clock on the morning of May 22, Stone moved his regiment out of the breastworks and down into the ravine and there arranged it for the assault, with two companies out in front as skirmishers. The 21st Iowa under Major Salue G. Van Anda moved out behind the 22nd, ready to support its charge. To the left of the 22nd Iowa was Colonel Charles L. Harris's 11th Wisconsin, supported to the rear by the 97th Illinois of Landram's brigade. The latter two regiments were to aim their attack toward the rifle pits south of the redoubt.[15]

McClernand had assigned Hovey to oversee the preparatory artillery bombardment in this sector. Hovey had shown skill in handling artillery at Port Gibson and Champion Hill, and his division, which had seen hard fighting in the latter battle, was not slated to take part in this day's attacks. So he was a natural choice. Hovey deployed twenty-two guns to bear on the corner of the Railroad Redoubt nearest the Union lines. About 6 A.M., the gunners opened fire. After four hours of pounding, the guns had battered a small gap in the corner of the Confederate earthwork, throwing enough dirt into the ditch to fill it at least partially.[16]

Promptly at 10 A.M. Lawler's brigade surged up the side of the ravine. In the lead, the 22nd Iowa swept over the rim onto the relatively gentle slope that covered the last fifty to seventy-five yards to the redoubt.[17] To a Confederate watching from inside the redoubt, "the enemy . . . seemed to be springing from the bowels of the earth."[18] Nevertheless, the 22nd Iowa ran into a hail of bullets from the defenders in the redoubt and the adjoining trenches.[19]

The lay of the ground and the Confederate positions meant that this fire hit the left side of the 22nd's line harder than it did the right. The shape of the ridge it occupied dictated that the redoubt took the form of an irregular oval about seventy yards long and thirty yards wide with its long axis at about 45 degrees to the direction of Union advance. The redoubt's most vulnerable aspect was the rounded end that projected somewhat toward the Union position. This was the point the Union artillery had breached, and the Iowans advancing there were less exposed to Rebel fire. For the 22nd's left wing, however, the only way to approach the redoubt would be to swing to the right more than 90 degrees in order to come at the redoubt's long southwest side. Such a move would expose the attackers to a crossfire from both the redoubt and the adjoining trench line, which would then be on the attackers' left flank. Rather than charge into that murderous crossfire, the left wing, carrying the regimental colors, veered further left into another ravine that had its head about fifty yards south (to the Union left) of the redoubt. There the left of the 22nd Iowa found shelter at least from the fire of the redoubt.[20]

Nearby, the 11th Wisconsin and 97th Illinois were encountering similar difficulties. Cresting the western rim of the ravine in which they had sheltered before the attack, they surged forward across the relatively level ridgetop toward the Confederate rifle pit south of the redoubt only to discover that the ridgetop here was very narrow. As they charged forward, they abruptly found themselves plunging downhill into the same ravine in which the left wing of the 22nd Iowa was taking shelter just to the right of the 11th Wisconsin. The ravine was invisible from the Union lines. It was two hundred yards wide and just as deep as the one in which Lawler's troops had sheltered before the attack. It was choked with abatis and swept by Confederate fire. Struggling up the rough slope, through the tangled branches of the abatis, and under heavy fire, the 11th Wisconsin and 97th Illinois came to a halt.[21]

Meanwhile, Colonel Stone with the 22nd Iowa's right wing, which was under the immediate command of Lieutenant Colonel Harvey Graham, reached the ditch fronting the redoubt. Under heavy Confederate fire, some of the attacking troops took shelter on the ground. Others scrambled down into the ditch, especially where it was in part filled with earth blasted from the parapet by the Union artillery. Then they clambered up the other side to reach the parapet of the Railroad Redoubt.[22] From that vantage point they directed rifle fire against the defenders inside. Meanwhile, Sergeants Joseph E. Griffith and Nicholas C. Messenger, both of Company I, 22nd Iowa, led twelve men through the breach in the fort's earthen wall and into the redoubt.[23] There they engaged in hand-to-hand combat with some of the defenders.[24] The onslaught of Griffith and Messenger and their men, combined with the fire from the comrades along the parapet, drove the Rebel defenders out of this section of the redoubt.[25]

The interior of the redoubt was segmented by two lateral traverses—dirt embankments much like the fort's walls. These divided the interior of the redoubt into three separate areas, each surrounded on three sides by high dirt embankments and open on the fourth side, since the rear of the redoubt had no wall but was closed off by a Confederate rifle pit. The Rebels who fled the bayonets of Griffith's small squad and the fire of Graham's riflemen on the parapet retreated to the nearest traverse or to the rifle pit. The fire of Graham's men on the parapet and of their counterparts in the section of rifle pit opposite them turned the section of the redoubt between them into a no-man's-land. Griffith's small band could not advance to clear the rest of the redoubt, so they scrambled back through the breach and out of the redoubt to rejoin their comrades in the ditch.[26] The time was about 10:30 A.M.[27]

Stone remained outside the redoubt, choosing a position from which he could see both wings of his regiment as well as the Rebel works facing his men. He referred to his position as "the highest and most exposed point near the fort"—probably just outside the ditch near the southeastern corner of the redoubt.[28] By this time, the 21st Iowa had moved up in support of the 22nd. Its commander, Lieutenant Colonel Dunlap, was hobbled by a foot wound he had suffered at Port Gibson, three weeks before, and he had fallen behind during the advance. With the regiment halted in the shadow of the Railroad Redoubt, the limping Dunlap was able to catch up, and joined Stone on his high vantage point.[29]

Stone was ebullient. He mistakenly believed his men had full control of the redoubt and that the Rebels had abandoned their trenches between the redoubt and the railroad tracks. He also thought he saw Confederates retreating from the works to the left of the redoubt, the target of the 11th Wisconsin. In sum, he believed nearly all defenders had fled from an approximately five-hundred-yard sector extending southward from the railroad. They had, he thought, withdrawn over the crest of the ridge immediately behind their entrenchments and down into the next ravine between the entrenchments and the edge of the town, but he believed they had no entrenchments there or anywhere else between his troops and Vicksburg. Only a scattering of Rebel sharpshooters remained, he thought, concealed in the woods that lay just behind the Confederate entrenchments. To Dunlap, Stone exulted, "The door to Vicksburg [is] open."[30]

In fact, Stone was mistaken in some of his observations. The Confederate rifle pit south of the Railroad Redoubt was still very much manned by troops of the 20th and 46th Alabama regiments. The troops Stone saw at the edge of the woods just behind and above the rifle pit were in fact the nine infantry companies of Waul's Texas Legion, which Confederate general Stephen D. Lee, commanding the defenses in this sector, had ordered up in anticipation of a heavy Union attack here. The outlook for the attacking Federals was not nearly as good as Stone imagined.[31]

Stone and Dunlap were still standing on their vantage point, surveying the terrain and exchanging congratulations on the success of the assault, when a bullet struck Stone in the arm, and another hit Dunlap in the head. Stone believed both shots had come from the sharpshooters in the woods to their left front, just beyond the line of the Rebel rifle pit.[32] Those would be the men of Waul's Texas Legion. Dunlap was killed, but Stone continued for a time to exercise command of his regiment.[33] He wanted a flag planted on the parapet of the redoubt, but the 22nd's was still down in the ravine to the left along with the left wing of the regiment.[34] So he turned to the 77th Illinois Regiment.

With Lawler's brigade stalled at the front of the Railroad Redoubt, Colonel William J. Landram's brigade of A. J. Smith's division had moved up to support the attack. By this time Landram's troops were sheltering in the ditch or along the outer slope of the redoubt's earthen walls along with Lawler's men. The 77th Illinois, one of Landram's regiments, was hunkered down very close on Stone's left.[35] So Stone sent an order for the 77th's color-bearer to bring up his flag, and when he did Stone had it planted atop the earthwork. By about 11 A.M., the 22nd's own color guard brought their flag up out of the ravine to join the 77th's on the parapet.[36] Around noon Stone's wound finally forced him to leave the field.[37]

Back on the Union breastworks, Lawler could see signs that the enemy in his front was also receiving reinforcements from the unengaged part of the line farther south. Those reinforcements were of course Waul's Texans. So Lawler thought it best to order his troops merely to hold on to what they had. He hoped he would receive more reinforcements from other sectors so that he could resume his advance, but his and Landrum's men continued to wait through the rest of the morning and into the afternoon.[38] Confederates along the rifle pits to the right and left of the redoubt kept the troops in the ditch pinned down with crossfire, while in the sections of the redoubt still in Confederate hands, the defenders hurled hand grenades over the parapet and into the ditch.[39]

While the fight continued along the parapet and ditch of the Railroad Redoubt, McClernand at 11:15 A.M. penned a message to Grant: "I am hotly engaged with the enemy," he wrote. "He is massing on me from the right and left. A vigorous blow by [James B.] McPherson would make a diversion in my favor." But the Confederates were not massing against the Thirteenth Corps from the sectors of McPherson's Seventeenth Corps. Local Confederate reserves, Waul's Legion, were sufficient to hold the line in McClernand's front. At 11:50 A.M. Grant wrote his response: "If your advance is weak, strengthen it by drawing from your reserves or other parts of the lines." Grant was apparently unaware that McClernand, unlike the army's other two corps commanders, had not maintained a significant reserve.[40] Yet McClernand declined to commit even the one brigade he did have.

By the time he received Grant's dispatch, McClernand was even more convinced that he was winning a great victory and ought to have the support of the whole Army of the Tennessee. At 11:46 A.M., as an officer of the Thirteenth Corps staff remembered, another officer (not named in the report) reached McClernand's command post with the news that the Railroad Redoubt was now in Union hands and asking that the Federal batteries cease firing on that work. McClernand was at first incredulous and sent Captain F. H. Mason of his staff to consult Landram as to whether this was so. Landram assured the captain that it was so and, as Mason recalled three months later, showed him a note from Graham stating that it was written inside the enemy fort.[41] It's not clear, however, that Graham actually was in the redoubt. Accounts of Federals inside the work all limit the attackers there to Griffith and his squad.

At any rate, McClernand responded to Grant's missive with another of his own: "We have gained the enemy's intrenchments at several points, but are brought to a stand," he stated, adding, "My troops are all engaged, and I cannot withdraw any to re-enforce others." He urged that a division of McPherson's corps be ordered to support him.[42]

At noon, McClernand again wrote to Grant: "We are hotly engaged with the enemy. We have part possession of two forts, and the Stars and Stripes are floating over them. A vigorous push ought to be made all along the line."[43]

Back came a dispatch from Grant reiterating that McClernand was free to draw in Brigadier General John McArthur's division, an element of McPherson's corps that had previously moved around to extend McClernand's line farther to the left. "Sherman and McPherson are pressing the enemy," Grant explained. "If one portion of your troops are pressed, re-enforce them from another. Sherman has gained some successes."[44]

In fact, Sherman's successes were more limited than McClernand's, but Grant assumed McClernand could do what Grant himself had done at Champion Hill—pull troops from a less hard-pressed sector of the line to one that was more heavily engaged. McClernand could not, however, and McArthur's division was too far away to be of timely assistance.

On the whole, Grant was skeptical about McClernand's claims of meaningful success. From his own vantage point on a high hill near the center of the Union line, he could not see any indication of a significant breakthrough in McClernand's sector or anywhere else. What he did see were clouds of white powder smoke continuing to rise all along the line, including from the area of the Railroad Redoubt—sure indication that the Confederates were still stoutly resisting McClernand's attack. Still, if somehow McClernand really had scored a breakthrough or had a good opportunity for one, it would be a shame not to support him. At 2 P.M. Grant ordered Sherman and McPherson to renew their attacks and directed McPherson to send Brigadier General Isaac F. Quinby's division to reinforce McClernand, whom he notified of this decision by a 2:30 P.M. dispatch. McClernand replied in a 3:15 missive that he would renew his attack as soon as the reinforcements arrived and expressed confidence that he would sweep all before him.[45]

While the messages were traveling back and forth between McClernand and Grant, Confederate officers behind the Railroad Redoubt attempted to

organize a counterattack to drive off or capture the Federals clinging tena-
ciously to the fort's ditch and the outer slope of its walls, but Union fire cut
down key leaders and the counterattack disintegrated before it could get
moving. Subsequently Sergeant Griffith and his squad who had by this time
reentered the redoubt then rounded up a Confederate lieutenant and thirteen
Rebel enlisted men who had until then found shelter in the otherwise empty
section of the earthwork swept by the Iowans' fire.[46]

Around 2 P.M., Lawler sent a dispatch back to McClernand: "The enemy
are massing their forces in our front. No movement of our troops on our
left. We ought to have re-enforcements."[47] The troops on the left to which
Lawler referred were the division of Major General Peter J. Osterhaus, also
of McClernand's Thirteenth Corps. Lawler seems to have been suggesting
that if Osterhaus's troops were not accomplishing anything where they were,
some of them, at least, ought to be shifted to the right to strengthen the
attack on the Railroad Redoubt. This move was consistent with what Grant
had written to McClernand a short time before, but the latter apparently
still deemed it impracticable.

At 2:40 P.M., Landram sent a dispatch of his own to his division commander, A. J. Smith: "Our men are holding the flanks of the fort in our
front. There is a heavy cross-fire upon us, and we have lost many killed and
wounded. They are hurling hand-grenades upon us, and hurting us consid-
erably in that way."[48]

One of Landram's soldiers, William Wiley of the 77th Illinois, later noted
that throughout this stage of the fight, the Confederates made a number of
bids to seize his regimental colors, which had been planted on the parapet.
Union riflemen both in the ditch and on the ground farther back from the
redoubt shot down several Rebels attempting to snatch the flag. Wiley had
to admit, though, that his comrades in the ditch were having a terrible time.
He agreed with his brigade commander that the grenades and lit shells were
the Confederates' deadliest weapons. Federals in the ditch began snatching
up the shells and throwing them back to explode inside the redoubt, which
for a time suppressed Rebel efforts. The Confederates eventually responded
by cutting the fuses extremely short. It was apparently possible to observe,
even as a shell bounced down the outer slope of the redoubt, the length of
the burning fuse, and when the Federals in the ditch saw one they thought
was about to burst, they pressed themselves flat against the ground and were
often able to escape injury. Ultimately, Wiley noted, "the only protection
the men in the ranks had was to make it so hot for the rebels that they were
afraid to raise their heads above the works to fire."[49]

It was about 3 P.M. when Quinby received Grant's order to march to the support of McClernand. He quickly withdrew his division from its position fronting the enemy and marched under the cover of an intervening ridge toward the Thirteenth Corps sector. A two-mile hike brought the division to McClernand's command post, where it arrived at about 4 P.M.[50] Inexplicably, McClernand sent one of its three brigades to Osterhaus's sector and only two to the general vicinity of the Railroad Redoubt. Of these two, one was to support the attack on the 2nd Texas Lunette and the other the Railroad Redoubt.[51] Even in response to the alleged breakthrough at the redoubt, McClernand was still distributing available troops along his line like a politician dispensing patronage.

McClernand assigned the brigade of Colonel George B. Boomer to the sector of the Railroad Redoubt, but he gave Boomer orders to assault the line of trench north of the railroad, between the redoubt and the 2nd Texas Lunette. Boomer led his troops forward across a narrow ridge under heavy fire. Short exposure kept losses relatively small, and the brigade soon scrambled down into a ravine in front of the Rebel works. Like the ravine in which Lawler's troops had sheltered before the start of the attack that morning, this one was deep and steep enough to give the men of Boomer's brigade cover from the fire of Confederates in the rifle pits in front of them and from the 2nd Texas Lunette, on their right front. They were, however, exposed to any fire that might come from the direction of the Railroad Redoubt, 250 yards away on their left front. Boomer reckoned they had little to fear from that direction, though, since by this time the flag of the 48th Ohio had joined those of the 77th Illinois and 22nd Iowa on the redoubt's parapet. Clearly, that work was in friendly hands. So Boomer halted his troops in the bottom of the ravine to regroup in preparation for a final rush toward the Rebel rifle pit.[52]

Unfortunately for Boomer, events at the Railroad Redoubt were even then taking a different turn. Confederate general Stephen D. Lee, commanding this sector of the defenses, had become concerned about the small but lingering Federal lodgment just inside the edge of the redoubt as well as the fact that one of the redoubt's three sections was a no-man's-land. Eager to reclaim full control of the fortification before U.S. reinforcements could lend further weight to the attack, Lee asked Colonel Waul to launch a counterattack. Since space was limited within the redoubt, Waul assigned the job to a small detachment of his command—about forty men. It was a little after 5:30 P.M. when the Texans clambered out of the rifle pit that faced the open base of the redoubt and charged toward the small knot of Iowans still holding out in the corner of the fort near the breach in the wall. Outnumbered more than three to one, the Federals had no chance. All were killed or captured except Sergeant Griffith, who scrambled back through the breach to the relative safety of the ditch outside the redoubt.[53]

The Rebels were not finished though. They surged up the inner slope of the wall to emerge atop the parapet and begin firing down into the U.S. troops sheltering in the ditch. They captured the flag of the 77th Illinois there atop the parapet and shot down the last of the color guard of the 22nd Iowa just outside the ditch, so that a Confederate patrol that evening was able to pick up that flag too. Only the 48th Ohio's colors escaped. The men in the ditch fared little better, as the Rebels lashed them with rifle fire and hurled grenades and artillery shells (their fuses lit) down into the men huddling in the ditch. Presently, a wounded Lieutenant Colonel Graham and fifty-eight members of the 22nd Iowa surrendered.[54]

It was about this time that Boomer was arranging his brigade in a column of attack in the ravine about 200 to 250 yards to the northeast of the redoubt. He was about to give the order to advance when a volley of fire from Rebels on the parapet of the Railroad Redoubt struck him down. He died only a few moments later and with his last breaths urged his successor, Colonel Holden Putnam of the 93rd Illinois, to call off the attack. Putnam wisely did so.[55]

Firing ceased as darkness fell, and at 8 P.M. Carr gave orders for the attacking troops, who had hitherto been clinging to what shelter they could between the lines, to make their way back to the positions they had held the previous evening. "Darkness never was more acceptable," wrote Wiley of the 77th. In Lawler's brigade, casualties totaled 375 killed, wounded, and missing. The toll was worst in the 22nd Iowa, which lost 164 men including its colonel and lieutenant colonel. It was the highest loss for any Union regiment that day.[56]

McClernand's claims of success at the Railroad Redoubt and demands to be reinforced by the rest of the army were bitterly resented by most of the army's officers. Later that night many of the corps and division commanders gathered at Grant's headquarters and spoke bitterly of McClernand. Army of the Tennessee chief of staff John A. Rawlins said angrily that McClernand's claims of a partial breakthrough amounted to a blunder that had cost the army one thousand lives to no purpose. Colonel John Sanborn, who commanded the brigade of Quinby's division that McClernand launched against the 2nd Texas Lunette, put the number of wasted lives at two thousand. Actually, Rawlins's number was closer to the truth, but even then only as to the total of killed, wounded, and missing—not the number of outright dead. Total Union casualties for the assault came to just over three thousand men, and a third of them likely fell after the renewal of the assaults in response to McClernand's demands.[57]

The men in the ranks held views similar to their generals'. Charles D. Morris of the 33rd Illinois believed McClernand simply had not been able to see how tenuous was his men's hold on the Confederate fortifications. He and other soldiers also wondered why McClernand had not committed the unengaged brigade of Hovey's division. If he had, Morris believed, "we would have broken their line."[58]

Participants with slightly more rank were not necessarily as sure of the potential for success with that level of reinforcement. Major J. B. Atherton, who took over command of the 22nd Iowa that evening after Lieutenant Colonel Graham was captured, wrote a few weeks later, "[H]ad we been re-enforced by two *divisions* when in possession of the fort, we would have held it, forced our way through the enemy's works, and driven them from our right and left" (emphasis in the original).[59] Reinforcements on that scale simply were not available in any sector of the front, and the major undoubtedly knew it.

By and large, the critics of McClernand throughout the army and in his own corps were right. McClernand and several of his subordinates, notably Colonel Stone of the 22nd Iowa, had been mistaken about the degree of their success against the Railroad Redoubt. The breakthrough there had never been more than minimal in scale. There were never more than a dozen or so Iowans inside the earthwork, and they were facing stout Confederate defenses in the trench behind the fort's open rear face. Also, Stone underestimated the size of the unbroken Confederate forces in his front. Waul's Texas Legion was still very much battle-worthy, as were the Alabama regiments deployed in the immediate vicinity of the redoubt. In fairness, Stone was making his assessment in the smoke and confusion of battle, under heavy enemy fire, and in a situation that still seemed to be quite fluid. His error is entirely understandable, and its nature reflects the optimistic, aggressive style of thinking that characterized the Army of the Tennessee and helped make it formidable.

Turning the Iowans' tiny incursion into a significant breakthrough would have taken major reinforcements promptly committed within a fairly brief interval after the initial success. But troops could not be moved from the other two corps of the Army of the Tennessee in time to reinforce the assault on the Railroad Redoubt before the Confederates could match the move with reinforcements of their own. The only real chance for success would have lain in McClernand reducing the assault on the Square Fort to a one-brigade feint. That would have given him a two-brigade reserve. Such a reserve could have been held ready opposite the Railroad Redoubt and then could have moved quickly to exploit any success by the initial attackers. Even then, success would not have been guaranteed. The defenders of Vicksburg had great advantages against any assault. It may be that Major Atherton was right and that it would have taken two additional divisions to break through the defenses. That meant Vicksburg simply could not be taken by assault, given the numbers of troops and the tactical situation that prevailed in late May.

Notes

1. Edwin C. Bearss, *The Campaign for Vicksburg*, vol. 3, *Unvexed to the Sea* (Dayton, OH: Morningside, 1986), 800; Warren E. Grabau, *Ninety-Eight Days: A Geographer's View of the Vicksburg Campaign* (Knoxville: University of Tennessee Press, 2000), 376.

2. Bearss, *Unvexed to the Sea*, 803–4.

3. Grabau, *Ninety-Eight Days*, 376.

4. U.S. War Department, *The War of the Rebellion: A Compilation of the Official Records of the Union and Confederate Armies*, 128 vols. (Washington, DC: Government Printing Office, 1880–1901), series 1, vol. 24, pt. 2: 140. Hereinafter cited as *OR*.

5. *OR*, vol. 24, pt. 2: 138; Jeffry Burden, "Into the Breach: The 22nd Iowa at the Railroad Redoubt," *Civil War Regiments* 2 (1992): 24.

6. *OR*, vol. 24, pt. 2: 130.

7. *OR*, vol. 24, pt. 2: 139.

8. *OR*, vol. 24, pt. 1: 151; pt. 2: 135–39; John Sewell, "The 77th Ill. at Vicksburg," *National Tribune*, June 3, 1893, 3.

9. Bearss, *Unvexed to the Sea*, 785.

10. Burden, "Into the Breach," 25; *OR*, vol. 24, pt. 2: 242; Colonel William M. Stone of the 22nd Iowa estimated the ditch to be ten feet deep and six feet wide and the walls to be twenty feet high. *OR*, vol. 24, pt. 2: 244.

11. *OR*, vol. 24, pt. 1: 178.

12. Ibid.

13. Ibid.

14. Ibid.; Burden, "Into the Breach," 27–28.

15. Bearss, *Unvexed to the Sea*, 824; *OR*, vol. 24, pt. 1: 178; pt. 2: 140, 242, 244.

16. Bearss, *Unvexed to the Sea*, 823–24; Burden, "Into the Breach," 27; Grabau, *Ninety-Eight Days*, 376. Grabau puts the number of guns under Hovey's direction at twenty-four.

17. *OR*, vol. 24, pt. 1: 178; pt. 2: 140–42, 242–43.

18. Bearss, *Unvexed to the Sea*, 824.

19. *OR*, vol. 24, pt. 1: 178; pt. 2: 140–42, 242–43; Bearss, *Unvexed to the Sea*, 824.

20. *OR*, vol. 24, pt. 1: 178.

21. *OR*, vol. 24, pt. 2: 141; Burden, "Into the Breach," 28.

22. *OR*, vol. 24, pt. 1: 178, 180; pt. 2: 140–41; Bearss, *Unvexed to the Sea*, 825.

23. *OR*, vol. 24, pt. 1: 178, 180; Bearss, *Unvexed to the Sea*, 825.

24. Grabau, *Ninety-Eight Days*, 377; *OR*, vol. 24, pt. 1: 178, 180.

25. Grabau, *Ninety-Eight Days*, 377; Bearss, *Unvexed to the Sea*, 825.

26. *OR*, vol. 24, pt. 2: 140–41, 154–55; Samuel C. Jones, *Reminiscences of the Twenty-Second Iowa Volunteer Infantry* (repr., Iowa City, IA: Press of the Camp Pope Bookshop, 1993), 38; Bearss, *Unvexed to the Sea*, 742; Grabau, *Ninety-Eight Days*, 375–77.

27. *OR*, vol. 24, pt. 1: 178–79.

28. Ibid., 178.

29. *OR*, vol. 24, pt. 1: 178; pt. 2: 140–42, 240–41.

30. *OR*, vol. 24, pt. 1: 178; pt. 2: 140–42, 240–41; Burden, "Into the Breach," 28.

31. Bearss, *Unvexed to the Sea*, 824–26.

32. *OR*, vol. 24, pt. 1: 178.

33. *OR*, vol. 24, pt. 1: 178; pt. 2: 140–42, 240–41.

34. *OR*, vol. 24, pt. 1: 178, 181; pt. 2: 140–41.

35. *OR*, vol. 24, pt. 1: 177; Sewell, "77th Ill. at Vicksburg," 3.

36. *OR*, vol. 24, pt. 1: 178–79, 181; pt. 2: 140–41.

37. *OR*, vol. 24, pt. 1: 178; pt. 2: 140–42, 242–43.

38. *OR*, vol. 24, pt. 2: 141.

39. *OR*, vol. 24, pt. 1: 177.

40. Ibid., 172.

41. Ibid., 181.

42. Ibid., 172.

43. Ibid.

44. Ibid.

45. Ibid., 173; Bearss, *Unvexed to the Sea*, 837; Grabau, *Ninety-Eight Days*, 378; Burden, "Into the Breach," 31.

46. Bearss, *Unvexed to the Sea*, 827; Grabau, *Ninety-Eight Days*, 377; *OR*, vol. 24, pt. 1: 178, 180.

47. *OR*, vol. 24, pt. 1: 177.

48. Ibid.

49. William Wiley, *The Civil War Diary of a Common Soldier*, edited by Terrence J. Winschel (Baton Rouge: Louisiana State University Press, 2001), 51; Burden, "Into the Breach," 33.

50. *OR*, vol. 24, pt. 1: 732; Bearss, *Unvexed to the Sea*, 847; McClernand reported the time as "about 5 o'clock." *OR*, vol. 24, pt. 1: 617. Time discrepancies of this magnitude are common in first-hand accounts of Civil War battles.

51. Bearss, *Unvexed to the Sea*, 847.

52. Ibid., 848–49; Grabau, *Ninety-Eight Days*, 378–79.

53. *OR*, vol. 24, pt. 2: 141–42, 243; Wiley, *Civil War Diary*, 51–52; Bearss, *Unvexed to the Sea*, 849–51.

54. *OR*, vol. 24, pt. 1: 179; pt. 2: 141–42, 243; Bearss, *Unvexed to the Sea*, 851.

55. Bearss, *Unvexed to the Sea*, 851–52.

56. *OR* vol. 24, pt. 2: 141, 161, 242, 244; Burden, "Into the Breach," 33.

57. William L. B. Jenney, "Personal Recollections of Vicksburg," *Military Essays and Recollections: Papers Read before the Commandery of the State of Illinois, Military Order of the Loyal Legion of the United States* (Chicago: Dial Press, 1899), 12: 261 (hereinafter *MOLLUS*); John B. Sanborn, "The Campaign against Vicksburg," in *MOLLUS*, 27: 134; Wiley, *Civil War Diary*, 52.

58. Charles D. Morris, "The Charge at Vicksburg," *National Tribune*, April 16, 1885, 3; John Quincy Adams Campbell, *The Union Must Stand*, edited by Mark Grimsley and Todd D. Miller (Knoxville: University of Tennessee Press, 2000), 99–100.

59. *OR*, vol. 24, pt. 1: 179.

4

TEXANS IN THE BREACH: WAUL'S
LEGION AT VICKSBURG

Brandon Franke

Vicksburg, Mississippi, is situated atop one-hundred-foot bluffs overlooking the Mississippi River. Because of its strategic location, there
were numerous Union attempts to wrest Vicksburg from Confederate hands.
If the North could control Vicksburg, it would ultimately control the great
river, effectively cutting the Confederacy in two, hindering the movement of
Rebel troops and supplies from one theater to another, and thus shortening
the Rebellion. All the Union attempts to take Vicksburg failed, except one.

Prior to Major General Ulysses S. Grant's decision to lay siege to the city,
the last attempt to wrench it from Confederate hands occurred on May 22,
1863. Three corps of the Union army attacked the Vicksburg defenses in
vain. Confederate forces under the command of Lieutenant General John
Pemberton denied the enemy a foothold within their fortifications in all but
one location. At the Railroad Redoubt, Federal forces successfully seized a
position within the Rebel defenses and would have secured it, if not for the
actions of Waul's Texas Legion. The Legion prevented Union forces from
establishing a stronghold within their line; as a result, Grant decided to lay
siege to Vicksburg, conceding that the city's defenses were too strong to
carry by force.

Organized in 1862 in Washington County, Texas, Waul's Legion consisted
of twelve companies of infantry, six of cavalry, and a battery of artillery.
Led by Colonel Thomas Neville Waul, a Texas lawyer and statesman, the
Legion was designed to have approximately two thousand soldiers. Legions
attempted to integrate the speed of cavalry, firepower of artillery, and mo-
bility of infantry all under one command. On paper, they seemed like independent commands capable of quickly attacking a target and escaping
before the Union army was able to retaliate. On the battlefield, they were
difficult to wield due to inherent difficulties in communicating with three

separate units and coordinating their movements. In addition, legions did not fit easily into the regimental, brigade, and divisional structures used by the majority of the Confederate army. When formed, they rarely served together, although they often retained their names when serving in different theaters. The original six-gun battery assigned to the Legion under Captain William Edgar was detached from the Legion in the fall of 1862 and assigned to the Trans-Mississippi Department under Brigadier General Henry McCulloch. Upon arrival in Vicksburg, Waul's cavalry would be reassigned to General Earl Van Dorn. Colonel Waul assigned Company G to train in artillery to compensate for the loss of Edgar's battery.[1]

Colonel Waul received orders to leave Camp Waul several miles north of Brenham, Texas, on August 7, 1862, and report to Little Rock, Arkansas. At that time the Legion numbered 1,559 enlisted men and 188 field and staff officers for a total of 1,747. Orders received on the march notified the Legion of a new assignment in General Van Dorn's Army of West Tennessee. Arriving in Vicksburg on January 2, 1863, the new commander of the city Lieutenant General John C. Pemberton placed Waul's Legion in Brigadier General William W. Loring's division.[2]

At the beginning of May 1863, Waul's Legion was encamped at a rude earthen rampart, dubbed "Fort Pemberton," that guarded the northern approach to Vicksburg on the Yazoo River. It was here that Colonel Waul received his orders to pull the Legion back to help defend Vicksburg. Reports of General John McClernand's Thirteenth Corps successfully crossing the Mississippi at Bruinsburg on April 30 had reached Pemberton, and he began marshalling all forces in his vicinity to protect the city. Pemberton's orders were to leave a small detachment at Fort Pemberton to guard the river but to make all haste to Vicksburg. Pemberton provided a steamboat at Yazoo City to expedite the Legion's return. On May 5, Waul's Legion marched toward Point Le Flore two miles to the east of Greenwood where the Tallahatchie River met the Yalobusha River. Company C of the First Battalion remained to defend Fort Pemberton and were still active when the rest of the Legion surrendered at Vicksburg. This group of Texans would later be mounted, retaining the name of the Legion.[3]

From Point LeFlore, the Legion marched south to Yazoo City, arriving at 4 P.M. on May 7. In the morning, they steamed south along the Yazoo River and arrived at Snyder's Bluff before the end of the day. The next stop was land overlooking Milliken's Bend, about two miles away from Vicksburg, on May 10. Second Lieutenant William A. Huckaby of Company B, 2nd Battalion, recorded in his journal that from this location he could see the Union Fleet on the Mississippi.[4]

Arriving at Vicksburg, the Legion discovered that General Pemberton had ordered the defensive perimeter of the city fortified in the Legion's absence. General Loring's army was serving as a shield between McClernand's Thirteenth Corps and the city. Therefore, when Waul's Legion arrived in Vicksburg, it was temporarily attached to Major General Carter Stevenson's division, most likely because of the proximity of the Legion to Stevenson, who at that point was guarding the rail line from Jackson to Vicksburg in the east as opposed to Loring's position in the south. As the Legion was already exhausted from traveling from northern Mississippi to Vicksburg, any assistance they could give to Loring would be insignificant. In the east they could rest and serve as reinforcements as needed.[5]

Huckaby detailed the next three days as quiet, with the Legion traveling through Vicksburg on May 11 and establishing a camp five miles east of the city after joining Stevenson's division. He reported on May 13 the reduction of his ration of bacon; already the Federal army's presence was causing the Confederates to conserve their supplies. Huckaby awoke to a rainstorm on May 14, the same day Major General James McPherson's Seventeenth Corps attacked Joseph E. Johnston's Army of Tennessee at Jackson. Unable to reinforce Pemberton, Johnston retreated north to Canton, leaving the Mississippi capital in the hands of the Union. Johnston, who outranked Pemberton, ordered Pemberton to vacate Vicksburg and march east with all available manpower. Pemberton was to strike Sherman's forces from the rear while Johnston launched a frontal attack, telling him "to beat such a detachment would be of immense value."[6]

Pemberton responded, informing Johnston that the available force of about sixteen thousand soldiers was marching to meet Johnston. Pemberton would leave behind Major Generals Martin Luther Smith and John H. Forney's divisions, numbering about seventy-five hundred men. "To this," Pemberton continued, "should have been Waul's Legion. . . . The men have been marching several days, are much fatigued, and, I fear, will straggle very much."[7] Much like Robert E. Lee at Gettysburg, Pemberton did not have a full understanding of Grant's intention or location, as he was without sufficient cavalry to provide a picture of the Union forces or their movements. Arriving at Edward's Depot two hours after departing Vicksburg, Pemberton discovered that what Johnston had labeled a "detachment" was in fact an entire army corps, leaving Pemberton vastly outnumbered. In addition, there was an equal-sized force on his right flank. Were he to continue as ordered, he would be forced to surrender Vicksburg. His consternation at this discovery prompted Pemberton to dispatch orders to General Forney to place Waul's Legion "in [a] position for the protection of Baldwin's Ferry road as soon as possible" to shore up Vicksburg's defenses.[8] The next morning, May 15, the Legion pulled back six miles to the Big Black River and established camp again. Pemberton ordered his troops to return to Vicksburg, realizing that joining forces with Johnston was no longer possible. While the Confederate soldiers retreated, the Union forces pursued them.[9]

Union General McPherson's Seventeenth Corps attacked the divisions of Generals Stevenson and John S. Bowen at Champion Hill on May 16. In his *Memoirs* Grant commended Pemberton's choice of location, noting that it, "whether by accident, or design, was well selected. It is one of the highest points in that section, and commanded all the ground in range."[10] During the battle, Pemberton ordered that General William Loring reinforce Stevenson's and Bowen's divisions. Loring refused, stating that his division was facing a stronger Union presence in General McClernand's advance from the south than initially expected. General Bowen's division counterattacked but fell short of defeating the Union forces due to lack of ammunition. As a result, Loring's division was cut off from Vicksburg by McClernand's forces, eventually joining Johnston in the north. The result of this battle was a confused and disorderly Confederate retreat to the Big Black River Bridge guarded by Waul's Legion.[11]

On the morning of May 17, Huckaby recorded in his journal that the Legion left camp for Vicksburg "in quick time" and that "considerable cannonading" from the direction of the Big Black River was heard. Here, Pemberton made his stand. He had ordered his forces to establish a line against the eastern side of the riverbank. Losing the Big Black River Bridge would prevent Pemberton's forces from maneuvering around Grant and would prevent Johnston from reinforcing him. Grant recounted that had Pemberton made a night march across the bridge, he could have "eluded us and finally returned to Johnston. But this would have given us Vicksburg."[12] Pemberton was not yet willing to surrender the "Gibraltar of the West." He had been charged by Confederate president Jefferson Davis "[t]o hold both Vicksburg and Port Hudson," as they were "necessary to a connection with the Trans-Mississippi."[13] It was imperative that Confederate forces hold the Big Black River Bridge. It was not to be.

A charge from McClernand's 2nd Brigade broke the Confederate line, and the Rebels retreated across the bridge. At 9 P.M., Waul's Legion arrived in their rifle pits at Vicksburg and camped near Warrenton Road, southeast of Vicksburg.[14] In the rush to get to Vicksburg, Major Maurice Kavanaugh Simons recorded in his journal, "We lost 33 pieces of cannon & several thousand men. Yesterday & today our men have been coming in very much demoralized. Our prospects are truly gloomy yet I have hope. . . . Good may yet come out of this."[15] Arriving before the retreating Confederate forces, Huckaby heard rumors of a severe engagement near the Big Black Bridge "in which the enemy are reported to have defeated our troops." In an attempt to preserve the routed army, "our troops burnt the R.R. bridge over Big Black," Huckaby recalled.[16] In his *Memoirs*, Grant wrote that had the Union forces prevented the destruction of the bridge, "I have but little doubt that we should have followed the enemy so closely as to prevent his occupying" Vicksburg.[17] Both Huckaby and Simons recorded the death of the much loved brigadier general Lloyd Tilghman, who was struck by a cannonball fragment in his chest. Amid what must have been a scene of disorganization and chaos during the retreat into Vicksburg, Huckaby calmly recorded the next day, "Slept tolerable well."[18]

The morning of May 18, General Pemberton set to the task of fortifying the defenses of Vicksburg. Waul's Legion received orders to change position from right to center, about two miles, to support General John Moore's brigade assigned there. Bivouacked in rear of Moore's brigade in a peach orchard, the Legion was to remain in reserve. Captain J. Q. Wall's Company B artillery was ordered to report to Forney's division and would remain attached to the division until the surrender of Vicksburg. At this point Waul's Legion consisted of eleven companies of infantry, a company of mounted scouts, and a battalion of Zouaves. At 6 P.M. Huckaby reported that a rumor was circulating throughout the camp that General Johnston had recaptured Jackson. He stated that this was "cheering news[,] we all have a [great] anxiety of the subject, some are very doubtful of success."[19] As well they should have been, as Johnston had not retaken Jackson, nor even made an effort to do so. During the day, Lieutenant Albert C. Lenert of Company E, Waul's Legion, reported "tolerable heavy firing" in the direction of Snyder's Bluff at 4 P.M.[20]

The fortifications to the extreme left of Huckaby began to receive fire at 2 P.M. on May 19. Believing his enemy demoralized, Grant had ordered an assault to gauge the enemy's defenses. Artillery was followed by small arms. During this engagement, the Legion was distributed to "different points on General Smith's and Forny's lines . . . or where the attack seemed imminent."[21]

Grant now was confident that his forces were as complete "as my limited number of troops would allow." Sherman's Fifteenth Corps was on his right, stretching to the Yazoo River, McPherson was in the center on the Jackson Road, and McClernand's forces held the left toward Warrenton as far as he could reach. Grant ordered Sherman to attack the northern defenses of the city to allow cover for the advancement of artillery and infantry. Lieutenant John Q. A. Campbell of the 5th Iowa Volunteer Infantry Regiment recalled that the "topography of country is very favorable to us" as the area surrounding Vicksburg was a "mass of hills jumbled together in every conceivable shape," thus allowing the placement of "batteries . . . along the brow of the hills while the infantry support finds a safe position back of the hills."[22] The same land that provided good terrain for the Federal forces to site their cannon and protect their infantry, however, also proved fortuitous for the defenders of Vicksburg. Elaborate Rebel fortifications established on the eastern edge of the city used those same topographical features so that attacking forces found themselves caught in a weave of interlocking fire while advancing and were forced to attack uphill from every approach.

Major General Stevenson placed the Legion in Brigadier General Stephen Dill Lee's Third Brigade. Lee's responsibility was holding the center of the Vicksburg line and the important railroad entrance into the city. In his official report, Waul stated the Legion was placed in that location, as it was "the most assailable and threatened point on General Stevenson's line."[23] Again, the Legion was to be held in reserve, left unused unless Lee's committed forces were overrun.

Beginning at 7 A.M., Union artillery fell throughout the rest of the day on the works to which Campbell recorded "the rebels responded spiritedly."[24] Lenert recorded that the day started slowly but "got hotter as the day commenced." At 10:15 A.M. the "enemy appeared in our front and commenced to fire on us. The minie [b]alls and [s]hells flying and exploding around us."[25] At 2 P.M. the area to the left of Waul's Legion began to receive concentrated fire, which, according to E. W. Krause, fell "like sleet."[26] Shortly afterward, Lenert recalled a courier traveling "at full speed" with orders for the Legion to reinforce Lee's left as "they were fearful the enemy would over-power them." With what may seem a bit of theatrical flair, Lenert recounted that "the Colonel [Waul] came charging up on his horse and before some could get ready, ordered us by the left flank DOUBLE QUICK MARCH!" The path that the Legion took was between two hills with limited cover. There "the Federals could make good targets of us, and they sure rained bullets on us."[27] They had not traveled two hundred yards when they were ordered to return to camp. The Federal assault was repulsed three different times in succession, with Federal forces getting no closer than thirty yards from the Rebel trenches.[28]

The Union forces were probing the entire defensive line by 3 P.M., and thirty minutes later, Lenert reported, "musketry had checked up a little and the artillery on both sides were hard at work." Both he and Huckaby recorded that these exchanges became intermittent around 5 P.M. with sharpshooting on their right and "some cannonading" until 6 P.M. The fighting along their left continued until dark, when skirmishing among the pickets and firing from mortar boats below Vicksburg replaced it.[29]

That evening, General Smith requested that Major R. W. Memminger, aide-de-camp to Major General Forney, direct Waul's Legion to him "in anticipation of an assault on my left in the morning" as "should the necessity for them arise, there will be no time to send for them."[30] At 11 P.M., the Legion received orders to form up to take up a position in the ditches to the left of William E. Baldwin's brigade along the northern fortifications at Fort Hill. Lenert recorded that this was "where the hardest fighting was during [night]."[31] Marching about a half mile to their new position, they discovered that the specified trenches were already occupied. They were then ordered to return to camp.[32]

By the end of the day, Campbell wrote in his diary that the Federal line "invests the rebel stronghold, from the Mississippi above to the Mississippi below Vicksburg." Nowhere had the Confederate line been penetrated. Grant's string of successes since crossing the Mississippi had broken apart on the Gibraltar of the West.[33]

Lieutenant Lenert's May 21 entry revealed that both sides had been firing at each other since daybreak. At 9:30 A.M. the fire from "artillery and musketry was steady." At noon, a light rain fell, but "this did not stop the fighting except on the firing on the river—it kept up." At dark, the Legion was ordered into its rifle pits. Lieutenant Campbell reported that the Federal mortars "have been throwing their huge missiles of destruction into the rebel stronghold" throughout the day.[34]

Once Grant had secured his supply lines, he dispatched orders for an assault for May 22. Information had reached him regarding General Johnston's similarly matched Army of Tennessee approximately fifty miles in the rear. Grant was determined to overwhelm Pemberton's forces and secure Vicksburg before finding himself between two armies. His next objective would be then to turn and drive Johnston from the state. Moving under the cover of Union artillery, the 22nd Iowa and other Union forces had advanced within striking distance of the Confederate fortifications. At 10 A.M. the general assault would commence.[35]

Artillery barrages from land and mortar fire from the river marked the start of the assault at 7 A.M. on May 22. After the cannonading stopped, all three Union corps attacked the city's fortifications. Waul reported "the enemy moved in distinct and separate columns against each of the salient points in General S. D. Lee's front."[36] The Second Brigade of the 14th Division of McClernand's Thirteenth Corps was tasked with attacking the Railroad Redoubt, a fortification that protected the southern side of the Southern Railroad of Mississippi. It was an earthen work in the shape of the letter J with the topmost portion running adjacent to the railroad track.[37]

Described by Captain Charles N. Lee of the 22nd Iowa, the redoubt was "surrounded by a ditch 10 feet deep, 6 feet wide, the walls being 20 feet high; the front subject to an enfilading fire of musketry and artillery from almost every direction."[38] In total, it covered half an acre of ground. Defending it were the 20th and 30th Alabama Infantry and three cannon. Major Oliver Steele of the Legion reinforced the redoubt with Second Battalion Company B and Company C. Joining the 22nd Iowa was the 77th Illinois, 130th Illinois, 21st Iowa, 19th Kentucky, and 48th Ohio. After the orders were given, Lenert recalled "WE DOUBLE QUICKED it over the hill and into the rifle pits." Upon arrival, the Legion found room along the trenches wherever it was available and proceeded to shoot at whatever target presented itself.[39]

The regimental historian of the 22nd Iowa, Lieutenant Samuel C. Jones, recounted the events of May 22: "About 9 am. [c]annonading commenced all around [our] line simultaneously. The Confederates replied, but not vigorously. . . . Hundreds of guns and mortars opened their mouths and belched forth flame and missiles of death." This bombardment lasted approximately an hour and fifteen minutes as "chasing shot and shell from both sides passed over [the 22nd Iowa]."[40]

Then, at 10:15 A.M., the rest of the 22nd Iowa "arose at once as if by magic out of the ground and charged the redoubt." They were within fifty yards of what the Union dubbed "Fort Beauregard." No sooner had they emerged from the ravine than they were fired on with grape and canister shot from cannons, which at that range, Jones recounted, "plow[ed] through our ranks."[41] Their objective was a hole in the fortification's salient that had been opened in the earthen walls by the artillery bombardment. To reach their target, they had to climb two hills that separated them from the redoubt. At the bottom of the first, they encountered "an almost impenetrable abattis" that broke their line and forced them to stop and re-form.[42] Once back in formation, they continued their advance up the last slope to the redoubt into a hail of withering fire. At the wall of the redoubt, the 22nd discovered it was too high to climb and that they had been not been provided with ladders. Still under fire, the men of the 22nd improvised. Sergeants Nicholas C. Messenger and Joseph Griffith along "with some fifteen or twenty men succeeded by raising one another up the wall."[43] Captain Charles Lee recorded that "fifty men of the Twenty-second scaled the walls and entered the fort, driving the enemy before them and taking 15 prisoners" and planting their regiment's flag on the inside of the redoubt.[44]

Although the 22nd Iowa was the first in the redoubt, they were not the first to plant their regimental flag. Albert Lenert was within twenty yards of the planting of the first flag, when he saw it "fluttering blue" on its pole. It belonged to the 77th Illinois.[45] Lenert recounted that a "boy in the Fort said they saw three Yankee flagbearers shot down" before they were able to successfully plant it in the fort's interior.[46] For this affront to Southern pride, Lenert recalled his commanding officer Captain J. A. Ledbetter "raised a shot at a yankee with his sixshooter, and they turned and [he] asked some of the boys to come. He would [show] them a yankee and [no] more than said this . . . he received a ball in his head killing him instantly." Sergeant Messenger later recorded that for his part in this initial exchange "I fired a few rounds in the fort [and] then [retired] to the outside as [did] most of the men who could get out."[47]

Fifteen minutes later, the 48th Ohio succeeded in planting their colors on the rampart as well. Three flagbearers were shot down before the 22nd Iowa was successful in planting "the Stars and Stripes" within the redoubt. Federal soldiers were able to take the first row of rifle pits within the redoubt but were unable to take command of the structure due to a second set of pits in the rear of it. They had no choice but to hope they were reinforced. A second Union charge to the left of Lenert's position was ineffective in assisting those in the redoubt, for "they were too weak."[48] In his official report, Charles Lee wrote that "it was impossible to hold [the redoubt] with such [an] inadequate force under a terribly destructive fire" due to the rear rifle pits.[49] In the ditch outside the redoubt, Lieutenant Colonel Harvey Graham ordered Sergeant Messenger to take a position on top of the earthen ramparts of the redoubt and continue firing on the Rebels. Messenger remained there four hours "under the floating stripes of the Gallant Old Flag."[50]

Facing a relentless assault over the entirety of his line by Union forces, General Lee placed the remainder of Waul's Legion in the center of the Vicksburg entrenchments to bolster the Confederate strength against the 11th Wisconsin and 97th Illinois. There, those in the line took horrendous losses as they were "unprotected by breastworks" and were subject to "galling fire," but as Waul later recounted in his letter to Major Memminger on July 30, 1863, they fought "with increased ardor, until the last of the enemy was prostrated or driven from their sight." So vicious was the fighting that the Legion's entire staff of officers was killed or injured.[51]

Having successfully repulsed the Union assault along their lines, the members of Waul's Legion discovered that a portion of the Railroad Redoubt was in the grip of Federal forces. Neither side had been able to secure possession of the earthen fort. At 12:30 "Alabamans (artillerists) threw 'hand-grenades' over into the Fort but the enemy held."[52]

To further Union control of the redoubt, General McClernand reported that "his troops had captured the rebel parapet in his front" and that reinforcements from General Grant were needed to secure it. McClernand had committed the entirety of his forces to the attack and had held nothing in reserve. According to General Sherman, after Grant read the request he turned to Sherman and declared, "I don't believe a word of it."[53] Sherman pressed his commanding officer that regardless of Grant's opinion of the letter or McClernand's fitness as a general, it was official and must be acknowledged. In his *Memoirs*, Grant stated that he was reluctant to accede to McClernand's request: "I occupied a position from which I believed I could see as well as he what took place in his front, and I did not see the success he reported. But his request for reinforcements being repeated I could not ignore it," but "his request for reinforcements being repeated I could not ignore it."[54] Grant ordered that Brigadier General Isaac Quinby's 7th Division of McPherson's corps reinforce McClernand and that McPherson and Sherman launch another attack as a diversion to Confederate attention on the redoubt.

Part of the 7th Division that would be sent to the redoubt as reinforcement was the 5th Iowa. Colonel George B. Boomer and the 5th Iowa arrived on the right of the redoubt at 5 P.M. Campbell commented that the request for reinforcements had arrived too late, as by that time they were "powerless for good." This would not stop General McClernand from trying to secure the Union's foothold on Vicksburg. Were he successful, the Federal forces would flood through the gap, flank Rebels on every side and take Vicksburg from the Confederacy. To this end, the 5th Iowa was joined by the 93rd Illinois in the front line, and a second line made up of the 26th Missouri and 10th Iowa.[55]

Campbell related that the approach to the redoubt was daunting: "In front of us were two ravines, and over this ridge we were ordered to charge, in order to reach the rebel works." At half past four, Colonel Boomer ordered his regiment to move out, "forward, common time, march." As soon as they reached the top of the ridge, they came within view of the Rebels and consequently were fired on by artillery and infantry in a devastating enfilading fire. The reinforcements were able to keep a "perfect line" to march down the slope of the first ridge toward their goal but had to stagger their line due to the nature of the terrain. From there they "double quicked the remainder of the distance into the ravine." At this point, they had been under fire for more than a minute, but "the balls flew about us like hail, and our loss was considerable."[56]

Lee's reports to Stevenson at 11:15 A.M. detailed the alarm he felt on the enemy's possession of the redoubt: "SIR: The enemy have been repulsed along my front; they have made a lodgement in the ditch of left work, and I have a stand of colors in the work. The work is full of our men. I cant reach them."[57]

Back at the redoubt, Colonel C. M. Shelley, commanding the 30th Alabama, and Lieutenant Colonel E. W. Pettus, commanding the 20th Alabama, had been unable to command their surviving forces to launch a counterattack to drive the Union soldiers from the front rifle pits of the redoubt. Aware of the ramifications were this foothold enlarged—the entire defense of Vicksburg could fall—Brigadier General Lee ordered the 30th and 20th to retake it, offering the flags to the command successful in doing so.[58]

Around noon Colonel Shelley raised a group of volunteers of the 30th Alabama to participate in a counterattack. Fifteen men led by Captain H. P. Oden and Lt. William Wallis assaulted the works from the gorge. Within moments both Oden and Wallis were killed along with several more soldiers. Nine soldiers were captured. Those that survived the hail of lead used whatever cover they could find to retreat.[59]

After receiving no response from Shelley or Pettus, Lee reiterated the order again. This time appealing to the honor of their battalions he offered them the enemy flags currently flying over the fort. After the last disastrous assault by the 30th Alabama no more volunteers appeared, regardless of "the more strenuous efforts of their chivalric commanders to urge or incite them to the assault."[60]

Lee then turned to Colonel Waul, who was at his headquarters, and directed the Legion to take the Railroad Redoubt and preserve the Confederate line. Waul took with him one battalion of the Legion to assist the assault and directed Captain L. D. Bradley and Lieutenant J. Hogue, already at the redoubt, to choose twenty men from Company B and fifteen from Company C.[61]

As Bradley was requesting volunteers to assault the fort, Lieutenant Colonel Pettus of the 20th Alabama approached him. In a letter to Rufus Hardy written in 1907, Pettus recounted his conversation with Bradley. "He [Bradley] said, 'Did you see that Alabama company killed, trying to take [the Redoubt]?' I answered, 'Yes, I saw it, but the captain and all his men were killed before they got to the back door of the redoubt; I expect to kill them before they know we are coming.'" Bradley and Hogue called for volunteers to go with him Bradley to take the redoubt, hoping to get thirty men. Pettus recounted that the entirety of both companies volunteered. Bradley then stated that he wanted no married men to take part in this action, to which his second lieutenant William M. High responded, "Captain, you are a married man; let me lead the troops." Bradley replied, "No; where my troops go, I lead them."[62]

With the men selected, Pettus announced that he would lead them in the assault, as he was the highest-ranking member there, and that he had intimate knowledge of the terrain, as his own men had been assigned to protect the redoubt. This was objected to by the men of Waul's Legion, declaring that as they were Bradley's men, they must be led by him. To this, Pettus "waived his superior rank" and said "we will go together." Three men

from the 30th Alabama would join them. They approached the rear of the
redoubt by a "circuitous" route, which led them away from their goal until
they were out of sight of Federal forces. Once that was accomplished, they
reversed direction and traveled by way of the Confederate trenches "heads
down and out of sight" until they reached the redoubt.[63]

During this time, Corporal Isaac H. Carman of the 48th Ohio Infantry,
Company A, had secured a position in the front rifle pits of the redoubt with
a man from Illinois in a hole beneath him that had been created by an ex-
ploded shell. This man reloaded their rifles while Carman fired each at any
rebel who came within range. This arrangement lasted several hours until
rebel shelling of his position made the position untenable. Carman slunk
back into the ditch, but the flags still flew.[64]

Arriving at the rear entrance to the redoubt, Pettus pulled from his pocket
a red bandanna that was the agreed-upon signal for the Confederates in the
rear rifle pits to stop firing. It was 5 P.M. when Pettus dropped the bandana. The
firing ceased, and Pettus, Bradley, and their thirty-eight volunteers stormed the
rear of the redoubt. Pettus recalled that the battle lasted "a few seconds time"
and "those in the redoubt and at the back door were disposed of." Not one
of the Legion sustained an injury in this assault, but two overzealous Texans
pursued the fleeing Union soldiers to the front of the redoubt and "fired over
the broken walls at the Federals on the outside, and in so doing were shot
in the face, but not seriously hurt."[65] With the Union soldiers driven back,
the men of the Legion turned to the enemy flags flying in their fortification.

Corporal Carman noticed the arrival of Pettus and the Legion. He requested permission to retrieve the 48th Ohio's flag to prevent its capture.
He was able to grab it before the counterattack began, but "the [77th] Illinois
standard could not be saved."[66] In his haste to get back to his own lines,
Carman impaled himself on a fellow soldier's bayonet but was still able to
prevent the capture of his regiment's flag. By this time, the 77th Illinois's
regimental standard had flown over the Railroad Redoubt for nine hours. So
many bullets had been fired in its vicinity that it had been shot off its staff,
and the flag itself was in shreds, "falling into the ditch, where it was buried
by earth by some our wounded men when, they saw the rebel rush."[67]

Pettus recounted after the counterattack that the "floor of the redoubt
was more than covered by dead soldiers—Confederates and Federals." He
ordered the men to get to cover, and as they did "a large number" of Federal
guns opened fire on the retaken fort. There were still numerous Federals in
the ditch on the other side of the redoubt. Pettus ordered them to surrender,
but they refused. Eventually, the Legion convinced them to "raise 'white rag'"
by dropping "hand-grenades" into the ditch.[68] Lieutenant Colonel Harvey

Graham of the 22nd Iowa and upwards of thirty prisoners surrendered in this manner. Sergeant Messenger was hit by three bullets while on the parapet before he was pulled down to safety. Pettus recalled that after the Union soldiers' surrender it was necessary to compel them to come around the redoubt to prevent being caught in friendly fire when they tried to go through "portholes" blasted into the redoubt by Federal artillery. Lenert confirmed that "several were killed of the Yankees after they had surrendered from their own men, for during the time of the charge and after, the Yankees poured vollies [*sic*] of grape and canister but not a man of ours was killed in the charge but several were wounded."[69] After the redoubt was retaken, Pettus recalled that Captain Bradley tried to give the captured 77th Illinois flag to him, but he refused, stating, "It belongs to the Texans." Bradley accepted it.[70]

In response to the counterattack, the surviving members of the 22nd Iowa pulled their standard from the parapet and fled. But Lieutenant Colonel J. Wrigley and the men of the Legion's second battalion discovered the 22nd's flag on the ground, dropped by the fleeing Iowans. The victorious members of the Legion presented the captured 22nd Iowa's regimental standard along with the 77th's to Brigadier General Lee.[71]

After the assault, Captain Bradley was asked by one of his men,

> "What fellow was that that brought us into this hell's hole?" Bradley replied, "I don't know." To which the soldier stated, "That's a hell of a story, captain. Don't know his name or his rank?" The captain said "no, he did not" Thereupon the soldier replied with perfect freedom, "I move we elect him a Texan, name or no name, rank or no rank." And the captain put the motion to a vote, as though he was presiding at a town meeting, and I was unanimously elected "a Texan"—the greatest honor I ever received.[72]

While the counterattack was occurring, the 5th Iowa had reached the bottom of the ravine. They were able to see the 22nd Iowa driven from their position in the redoubt. Colonel Boomer was mortally wounded by a musket ball from their right flank as they approached the last hill. Campbell recorded his last words as "Tell Col. [Holden] Putnam (of the 93rd Illinois—our next senior Colonel) not to go over that hill."[73]

Colonel Putnam heeded the last command of Colonel Boomer. With the approach of evening, the likelihood of a successful attack continued to diminish. Putnam sent a dispatch to General Carr to relate their present situation and the loss of Colonel Boomer. Carr immediately responded that the division was to hold position until dark and then were to reform where they had begun their day.

The flags had floated over the Railroad Redoubt for ten hours. During the battle, Confederate troops captured other regimental flags, some placed on the outside fortifications marking the farthest extent of the Union's advance at Vicksburg. It was only at the Railroad Redoubt that Union soldiers succeeded in placing their colors within the Confederate lines. Had the men of Waul's Legion failed to drive out the Federal forces, the 5th Iowa and other reinforcements would have assuredly been able to widen their hold on the redoubt and pour behind the Confederate lines, thus changing the history of Vicksburg. To stave off another attack that evening, Waul reinforced Pettus, Bradley, and Hogue's victorious party with two more companies from the Legion. In a letter to Stevenson after the redoubt was secured, General Lee wrote, "GENERAL: The angle is carried and the enemy's colors taken. It was a gallant affair." In his report to General Pemberton, General Stevenson wrote of the counterattack by Waul's Legion and Lieutenant Colonel Pettus that a "more daring feat has not been performed during the war, and too much praise cannot be awarded to every one engaged in it."[74] The Legion had plugged the breach, preventing a sea of blue-coated soldiers from pouring through and washing away the Vicksburg's defenses.

In this assault, Grant's forces suffered 3,199 men killed, wounded, or missing. The total loss for McClernand's corps that attacked the area surrounding the railroad was 1,275. Casualties for Carr's division were 710, and those for Lawler's brigade, 368. The 22nd Iowa suffered 85 percent casualties. The Confederates lost no more than 500. Despite the Union's great loss of men, nothing was gained. Grant wrote in his *Memoirs*, "I now determined upon a regular siege to 'out-camp the enemy,' as it were, and to incur no more losses. The experience of the 22d convinced officers and men that this was best."[75]

The night of May 22, Pemberton and Waul visited the redoubt. Pemberton empowered Major General Stevenson to use any material he was able to find, including, "if necessary, by tearing up the railway" to reinforce the earthen embankments.[76] Pettus sent the captured flag to General S. D. Lee, who in turn sent it to Major General Stevenson, asking for permission to let the Legion retain it as promised.[77] Following the battle, Waul reported the status of the Legion: "Officers killed, 10; wounded, 37; missing, 1. Enlisted men killed, 37; wounded, 153; missing 7. Total number killed, wounded, and missing, 245."[78] As night fell the Legion took to burying its dead. E. W. Krause recounted that it was "2 o'clock when we buried the last one, who was our Adjutant." This was Louis Popendieck, who had been shot through the heart while standing beside Waul during the battle.[79]

The Legion stayed in the trenches during the next two days. A truce was declared on May 25 to allow for burial of the dead still on the fields that were rapidly decomposing in the May heat. Campbell was astonished that both sides allowed complete freedom of movement among their men, with soldiers from both sides "exam[ining] their works, and they came down and passed their remarks on our tunnels, and trenches."[80] William Bentley, recording the history of the 77th Illinois, referred to the day as a "social gathering" between the Union and Confederate soldiers, effectively a "social picnic."[81]

The Legion never gave up hope that Vicksburg would hold out until rescued. To maintain morale, Waul inquired of E. W. Krause, who served as bandmaster for the Legion, "if a little music would not be a good thing." Krause and the Legion band began to play "in a very patriotic air 'Dixie.'" Krause was incensed when the Union responded with "a very rude and unharmonious, double Forte accompaniment" along with their cannon "directed at the impudent bank in which we were sheltering." This continued until Waul ordered them to stop for the night. Krause wrote that this practice would continue throughout the siege, but as it wore on, an "excellent" Union band would respond to their playing of "Dixie" with "America."[82]

Lenert wrote in his diary on June 6 that reports that Johnston's Army of Tennessee had crossed the Big Black River and was preparing to attack Grant's forces had reached them. It was not to be; Johnston was amassing an army large enough to create a diversion to lift the siege, but would not be ready to attack until July 7. Johnston would notify Pemberton of this on July 3, but Pemberton would not receive this message until July 10, six days after he surrendered Vicksburg.[83]

For the forty-seven days of the siege of Vicksburg, the Legion and the rest of the Confederate army, along with its citizens, were subject to daily bombardment from land and river, and Union sharpshooters often struck their targets. On July 4, General S. D. Lee reported Union trenches were within "30 feet of our works." For "[t]he remainder of the siege the Legion was distributed in the rifle-pits and forts, forming nightly scouting parties, parties of reconnaissance, and supporting our working parties and pickets."[84] Trading continued between both sides during this time; Lenert recorded twice that "teamsters went to the Yankees from the Legion" once trying to obtain a batch of "Lincoln coffee."[85]

On July 4, Pemberton surrendered the Army of the Mississippi and the city of Vicksburg to General Grant. Colonel Thomas N. Waul gave this account of the men under his command: "At 10 o'clock of the day of the capitulation the command marched out of the intrenchments with the colors flying and band playing. Having saluted their colors, they stacked arms and returned—prisoners under parole—into camp."[86] After the surrender, the Union band that had engaged in a battle of songs with the Legion's band sought them out to "meet the band which had played in such unharmonious conditions." When they met, those men met not as enemies, but as fellow musicians, and upon seeing their starving conditions, provided a "good supply of provisions, such as crackers, sugar, bacon and flour, as well as the long missed luxury, coffee."[87]

The Union army paroled many of the men of the Legion after the surrender. Waul received his parole on July 17, 1863, and was promoted to brigadier general on September 18, 1863. He reformed the Legion as part of the Trans-Mississippi Department and ended the war on May 26, 1865.[88]

Notes

1. Marcus J. Wright and Harold B. Simpson, *Texas in the War, 1861–1865* (Hillsboro, TX: Hill Junior College Press, 1984), 128; Brandon Franke, "Waul's Texas Legion: Towards Vicksburg," *East Texas Historical Journal* 53, no. 1, 2, https://scholarworks.sfasu.edu/ethj/vol53/iss1/2/; Lester N. Fitzhugh, *Texas Batteries, Battalions, Regiments, Commanders, and Field Officers Confederate States Army, 1861–1865* (Salt Lake City, UT: Digitized by the Genealogical Society of Utah, 2008), 32; U.S. War Department, *The War of the Rebellion: A Compilation of the Official Records of the Union and Confederate Armies*, 128 vols. (Washington, DC: Government Printing Office, 1880–1901), series 1, vol. 13, 978. Hereinafter cited as *OR*. All references are to series 1 unless otherwise indicated.

2. Laura Simmons, "Waul's Legion from Texas to Mississippi," *Texana* 7 (1969): 4; *OR*, vol. 17, pt. 2: 824.

3. *OR*, vol. 24, pt. 3: 830–31; W. A. Huckaby, "Siege of Vicksburg, W. A. Huckaby, 2nd Lt., Bradley's Co., Waul's Legion," manuscript, and German letters and diaries from Waul's Texas Legion, Historical Research Center, Texas Heritage Museum, Hill College, Hillsboro, Texas.

4. Huckaby, *Siege*, 28. Although Huckaby does not specifically state that the Legion traveled by water, the trip today from Yazoo City to Snyder's Bluff by road is 37 miles. To travel that distance in so short a time implies that some method of transportation was employed. Pemberton's order to Waul dated May 4 indicating a steamboat would be available lends credence to this belief. In addition, Yazoo City served as the Confederate naval yard for the west indicates that some form of water transportation would be found.

5. *OR*, vol. 24, pt. 3: 852.

6. Ibid, vol. 24, pt. 3: 870.

7. Ibid, vol. 24, pt. 3: 877.

8. *OR*, vol. 24, pt. 3: 850, 878; John C. Pemberton, *Pemberton: Defender of Vicksburg* (Chapel Hill: University of North Carolina Press, 1942), 141, 145. Pemberton was desperate for cavalry, at one point requesting the return of the cavalry of Brigadier General James Ronald Chalmers that was originally part of Waul's Legion. Chalmers at that time was in Panola, Mississippi.

9. Huckaby, "Siege," 29; Pemberton, *Pemberton*, 152.

10. Pemberton, *Pemberton*, 163; U. S. Grant, *Personal Memoirs of U. S. Grant*, 2 vols. (New York: Charles L. Webster and Company, 1885), 1: 202.

11. Grant, *Memoirs*, 205; Pemberton, *Pemberton*, 160, 164; *OR*, vol. 24, pt. 2: 366.

12. Grant, *Memoirs*, 206.

13. Pemberton, *Pemberton*, 167.

14. A. C. Lenert, *Memorandum Book*, text, n.d., The Civil War and Its Aftermath collection, University of North Texas Libraries Special Collections, The Portal to Texas History, accessed March 27, 2017, texashistory.unt.edu/ark:/67531/metapth 160228/m1/7/.

15. Douglas L. Braudaway, "A Texan Records the Civil War Siege of Vicksburg, Mississippi: The Journal of Maj. Maurice Kavanaugh Simons, 1863," *Southwestern Historical Quarterly* 105, no. 1 (July 2001): 105.

16. Huckaby, *Siege*, 29.

17. Grant, *Memoirs*, 208.

18. Huckaby, *Siege*, 29; Braudaway, "Texan Records," 105.

19. Dupeire's battalion of Louisiana Zouaves had been attached to the Legion during the winter of 1862–63. They numbered 150 officers and men. Lenert, *Memorandum Book*, 2; Huckaby, *Siege*, 29; Janet Hewett, ed., *Supplement to the Official Records of the Union and Confederate Armies*, vol. 69 (Wilmington, NC: Broadfoot Publishing Company, 1994), 82; *OR*, vol. 24, pt. 2: 357; Edwin C. Bearss, *The Campaign for Vicksburg*, vol. 3, *Unvexed to the Sea* (Dayton, OH: Morningside, 1986), 735.

20. A. C. Lenert, *Memorandum Book*, 2.

21. Grant, *Memoirs*, 209; Huckaby, *Siege*, 29; Edwin C. Bearss, ed., "The Civil War Diary of Lt. John Q. A. Campbell," *Annals of Iowa* 39 (1969), 522, http://ir.uiowa .edu/annals-of-iowa/vol39/iss7/5; *OR*, vol. 24, pt. 2: 357.

22. *OR*, vol. 24, pt. 3: 922–27; Grant, *Memoirs*, 209; Robert A. Hasskarl, *Waul's Texas Legion, 1862–1865* (Ada, OK: Book Bindery, 1976), 21; Bearss, "Diary of Campbell," 522.

23. *OR*, vol. 24, pt. 2: 357.

24. Bearss, "Diary of Campbell," 522.

25. Lenert, *Memorandum Book*, 2.

26. Mamie Yeary, *Reminiscences of the Boys in Gray, 1861–1865* (Dallas: Smith and Lamar, 1912), 2: 412.

27. Ibid., 4.

28. Lenert, *Memorandum Book*, 2.

29. Ibid., 2; Huckaby, *Siege*, 29.

30. *OR*, vol. 24, pt. 3: 894.

31. Lenert, *Memorandum Book*, 2.

32. Huckaby, *Siege*, 29.

33. Braudaway, *Texan Records*, 523; Grant, *Memoirs*, 177, 209.

34. Lenert, *Memorandum Book*, 3; Bearss, "Diary of Campbell," 523.

35. Grant, *Memoirs*, 209; Samuel C. Jones, *Reminiscences of the Twenty-Second Iowa Volunteer Infantry* (repr., Iowa City, IA: Press of the Camp Pope Bookshop, 1993), 38. Jones indicates that on the morning of May 22 the 22nd Iowa was "along the edge of the ravine under the fort." John S. Kountz and Timothy B. Smith, *Record of the Organizations Engaged in the Campaign, Siege, and Defense of Vicksburg* (Knoxville: University of Tennessee Press, 2011), 41.

36. *OR*, vol. 24, pt. 2: 357.

37. Terrence J. Wincher, *Vicksburg: Fall of the Confederate Gibraltar* (Abilene, TX: McWhitney Foundation Press, 1999), 90.

38. *OR*, vol. 24, pt. 2: 243–45.

39. Guy E. Logan, "Historical Sketch Twenty-Second Regiment Iowa Volunteer Infantry," *Roster and Record of Iowa Troops in the Rebellion*, vol. 3, accessed May 10, 2017; *OR*, vol. 24, pt. 2: 354–55, 357; Hasskarl, *Waul's Texas Legion*, 22; Lenert, *Memorandum Book*, 4. Many sources state the 46th Alabama was assigned the redoubt. But Captain George Brewer of the 46th in his report stated that they had been relieved from duty and replaced in the trenches by the 20th Alabama. All officers and a portion of the 46th's staff were either captured or killed at Champion Hill. The 46th was brought up to reinforce Edmund Pettus's 20th already in the trenches on May 22.

40. Jones, *Reminiscences of the Twenty-Second Iowa Volunteer Infantry*, 38.

41. Ibid., 38.

42. *OR*, vol. 24, pt. 2: 351; Logan, *Historical Sketch*.

43. Logan, *Historical Sketch*; Nicholas C. Messenger, "Statement of Second Lieutenant Nicholas C. Messenger, Company I, Twenty-Second Iowa Infantry, on Operations in Vicksburg, Mississippi, May 21–28, 1863," *English Valley Star*, June 1, 2011, accessed May 11, 2017, http://www.hinkletown.com/evstarjune12011.pdf.

44. *OR*, vol. 24, pt. 2: 244.

45. Ibid, vol. 24, pt. 1, 178–79; Lenert, *Memorandum Book*, 4. Lenert states that it is a blue flag, thus the 77th Illinois Volunteers'. Charles N. Lee calls it the "Stars and Stripes," which was the template for the 22nd Iowa's and 48th Ohio's standard. A version of the 77th's is on display at the Missouri History Museum's website: http://collections.mohistory.org/resource/100665.

46. Lenert, *Memorandum Book*, 4.

47. Ibid., vol. 24, pt. 1, 178–79; Messenger, *Statement of Second Lieutenant Nicholas C. Messenger*; Lenert, *Memorandum Book*, 4.

48. Lenert, *Memorandum Book*, 4.

49. *OR*, vol. 24, pt. 2: 244.

50. Messenger, *Statement of Second Lieutenant Nicholas C. Messenger*.

51. *OR*, vol. 24, pt. 2: 357; Hasskarl, *Waul's Texas Legion*, 22.

52. Lenert, *Memorandum Book*, 4.

53. Ibid., vol. 24, pt. 2: 357; William T. Sherman, *Memoirs of General W. T. Sherman* (New York: Literary Classics of the United States, 1990), 352.

54. Sherman, *Memoirs of General W. T. Sherman*, 352; Grant, *Memoirs*, 210.

55. Bearss, "Diary of Campbell," 525.

56. Ibid., 526. Campbell states that it was half past seven when the 5th Iowa began their attempt to reinforce the redoubt. In the footnotes of this article, Bearss states that most sources say Colonel Boomer began his attack at 4:30.

57. *OR*, vol. 24, pt. 2: 349.

58. Ibid., vol. 24, pt. 2: 357.

59. Jeffrey C. Burden, "Into the Breach: The 22nd Iowa at the Railroad Redoubt," *Civil War Regiments: A Journal of the Civil War* 2, no. 1 (1992): 31.

60. *OR*, vol. 24, pt. 2: 350, 357. Lee would forward the flag to General Stevenson who in turn sent it to Pemberton.

61. Ibid., vol. 24, pt. 2: 358.

62. *Senate Documents*, vol. 17 (Washington, DC: Government Printing Office, 1909), 197, 201.

63. Ibid.

64. Walter F. Beyer and Oscar F. Keydel, *Deeds of Valor: How America's Heroes Won the Medal of Honor* (Amazon Digital Services, 2011), 1: 201–2.

65. Samuel D. Pryce and Jeffry C. Burden, *Vanishing Footprints: The Twenty-Second Iowa Volunteer Infantry in the Civil War* (Iowa City, IA: Camp Pope Bookshop, 2008), 117; Senate Documents, 201. Pettus and Lenert both recount that the Rebel counterattack that succeeded in taking the redoubt resulted in no deaths, and shots in the face to two men were the only injuries received in the assault.

66. Isaac Carman, "A Flag the Rebels Didn't Get," 48th OVVI—Cyrus Hussey Diary—Siege of Vicksburg, January 9, 2008, accessed May 17, 2017, http://www.48ovvi .org/oh48hd7.html.

67. Beyer and Keydel, *Deeds of Valor*, 201–2; *OR*, vol. 24, pt. 1: 179; William H. Bentley, *History of the 77th Illinois Volunteer Infantry, Sept. 2, 1862–July 10, 1865* (Peoria, IL: Edward Hine, 1883), 153. In Waul's report he comments that the flags flew for three hours, but the time involved from raising them to being captured gives credence to nine.

68. *OR*, vol. 24, pt. 2: 344; Lenert, *Memorandum Book*, 4.

69. Lenert, *Memorandum Book*, 4; Logan, *Historical Sketch*; Dave Jackson, "Three Cheers for Nick Messenger!," *English Valleys Star*, June 1, 2011, accessed May 11, 2017, http://www.hinkletown.com/evstarjune12011.pdf; Senate Documents, 202.

70. Senate Documents, 198.

71. *OR*, vol. 24, pt. 2: 357; Bearss, "Diary of Campbell," 537; Hasskarl, *Waul's Texas Legion*, 25.

72. Senate Documents, 202.

73. Bearss, *Diary of Campbell*, 526.

74. Jackson, "Three Cheers for Nick Messenger!"; Hasskarl, *Waul's Texas Legion*, 25; *OR*, vol. 24, pt. 2: 349, 351.

75. Logan, *Historical Sketch*; Wincher, *Vicksburg*, 93; Grant, *Memoirs*, 210.

76. Bearss, *Diary of Campbell*, 527; *OR*, vol. 24, pt.3: 915.

77. *OR*, vol. 24, pt. 2: 350; Hasskarl, *Waul's Texas Legion*, 25. Eventually the 22nd Iowa regimental flag was returned to Iowa. It is now part of the Iowa Civil War Battle Flag Project, http://www.hinkletown.com/evstarjune12011.pdf.

78. *OR*, vol. 24, pt. 2: 358.

79. Yeary, *Reminiscences of the Boys in Gray*, 412.

80. Bearss, *Diary of Campbell*, 527.

81. Bentley, *History of the 77th Illinois Volunteer Infantry*, 162.

82. Yeary, *Reminiscences of the Boys in Gray*, 412.

83. Lenert, *Memorandum Book*, 7; *OR*, vol. 24, pt. 1: 287.

84. *OR*, vol. 24, pt. 2: 351, 358.

85. Lenert, *Memorandum Book*, 6.

86. Lenert, *Memorandum Book*, 6; *OR*, vol. 24, pt. 2: 352, 358.

87. Yeary, *Reminiscences of the Boys in Gray*, 412.

88. Ernst August Franke, unpublished diary, family document. Hasskarl, *Waul's Texas Legion*, 38, 90; *OR*, vol. 24, pt. 3: 1011; Wright and Simpson, *Texas in the War*, 94.

Union major general John Alexander McClernand breached
Confederate lines at the Railroad Redoubt for most of the day during
the May 22 assault but was forced to retreat. Library of Congress

Union major general James Birdseye McPherson was one of Grant's corps commanders during the assaults of Vicksburg. Library of Congress

John Clifford Pemberton commanded the Confederate Army
of Mississippi that defended Vicksburg. Library of Congress

Ulysses Simpson Grant, commander of the Union Army of the Tennessee during the Vicksburg Campaign, hoped to capture the Confederate "City on the Hill" by assaulting their defensive lines. Library of Congress

Union major general William Tecumseh Sherman commanded one of Grant's corps during the assaults on Vicksburg. Library of Congress

Confederate colonel Thomas Neville Waul led a Texas legion on May 22 that reinforced the defensive lines and did not allow McClernand's soldiers to exploit the Railroad Redoubt breach. DeGolyer Library, Southern Methodist University, Lawrence T. Jones III Texas Photography Collection.

Ohio congressman Clement Vallandigham was the leading Copperhead of
the state and created a political controversy when he was court-martialed
and expelled from the North for opposing the war. Library of Congress

5

"THE NORTH-WEST IS DETERMINED WITH THE SWORD": MIDWESTERNERS' REACTIONS TO THE VICKSBURG ASSAULTS

Charles D. Grear

War conjures reactions from every participant, not just the soldiers in the ranks and the officers leading on the front lines but even civilians back home attempting to live their lives in the backdrop of conflict. People, both on the home front and in camp, constantly think of their friends and family members and worry about their safety and well-being. Civil wars tend to amplify the fear, death, and destruction that impacts all those with a connection to war. The American Civil War proved no different from any other. A soldier's connections range from those with the other soldiers in camp to relationships with loved ones sitting by the empty chair, waiting for his return. By focusing on the newspapers in the Midwest, particularly the smaller markets that have not received as much attention as larger ones, we can see the communities' reactions to the assaults of Vicksburg on May 19 and 22, their opinions of Ulysses S. Grant, and their economic, political, and social responses.

Civilians back home in the American heartland remained fixated on the events in Mississippi, as opposed to Robert E. Lee's offensive campaign in Virginia. Vicksburg was about as far from the Midwestern states as Lee was in Chancellorsville, Virginia, both cities being just over four hundred miles from the closest major city in the heartland. Despite the equal distance, people focused on Grant's actions along the Mississippi River.[1]

Midwesterners followed the western campaigns more closely because the bulk of the Federal regiments in the Vicksburg Campaign were from those states. The order of battle listed in *The War of the Rebellion: A Compilation of the Official Records of the Union and Confederate Armies* shows that 88 percent of the regiments were from the American heartland.[2] But

Midwesterners' participation in the Battle of Gettysburg, fought just over a month after the assaults, was nearly the opposite: only 13.4 percent of the regiments hailed from the heartland.[3] In addition, with control of the river at stake, the Vicksburg assaults would have a direct impact on the Midwestern economy. Opening the river to commercial traffic would again grant all Midwestern states, not just those bordering the Great Lakes, access to national and international markets. Newspapers from Kansas and Ohio concede these ideas. The editor of the *Grand Haven News* in Kansas commented, "By the latest intelligence we are informed that Vicksburg had not fallen into our hands, but that such a result is probable if not certain within a few days. The war news from all other directions is of but little interest or importance."[4] In Cleveland, Ohio, an editor pointed out, "In importance of results, no victory of the war has been of more value than this. Vicksburg, even more than Richmond, was valued by the rebels as a stronghold of Confederate power."[5]

With a string of victories across the state of Mississippi, ranging from Bruinsburg to Jackson to Big Black River Bridge to Benjamin Henry Grierson's Raid, the morale of Union forces was high. They found victory waiting at every engagement of the main thrust of the Vicksburg Campaign for nearly two months, March 29–May 18. Grant wanted to continue his attacks as they reached the outskirts of Vicksburg and ordered assaults of the Confederate defenses surrounding Vicksburg for May 19. Union troops were so confident that William Tecumseh Sherman authorized the 13th U.S. Infantry to include "First at Vicksburg" on their regimental colors.[6]

The assault on May 19 gained little ground for the Northern army, but the men celebrated what they could and held hope that victory was still around the corner. Though greatly exaggerated, a story in the newspaper *Urbana Union* from Ohio reported, "On the 19th the rebels were defeated at Haine's [sic] Bluff, with a loss of near nine thousand prisoners and one hundred pieces of artillery, mostly siege guns. On the 20th, there is reason to believe, the City of Vicksburg, with the remna[n]t of the rebel army, and the artillery they have been accumulating there for more than a year, fell into the hands of our victorious army."[7] Similarly, all the early accounts of the May 19 assault remained optimistic, with another recounting that the Union held key locations in Mississippi and gained Haynes Bluff "with every prospect of capturing the entire force in Vicksburg."[8] The accounts are overstating the accomplishments, since Confederates abandoned Haynes Bluff when General John C. Pemberton ordered their forces to consolidate around Vicksburg. No prisoners or guns were captured. With little information from the first assault, newspapers spun a positive report.[9]

As time passed, more details of the brutal fighting came to light and the tone of the accounts became darker. William M. Davis of the 95th Ohio Infantry, organized in Columbus, sent the *Daily Ohio Statesman* his "Rough Notes of a Soldier." For his May 19 entry on the brutal fighting at the Stockade Redan, he recorded, "Our brigade was much exposed. There was a large number killed and wounded. Two or three were wounded in the 95th, but none killed. . . . Many of our men were killed, owing to their curiosity in looking over the hill to see the fight. The firing ceased at dark."[10] Another member of the 95th Ohio wrote home describing his impressions of the assault. "It seems to have been at first the intention of our Generals to capture Vicksburg by storm; but that plan appears to have been abandoned, as it has proved to be utterly impracticable to mount the rebel works. We are still confident of eventually capturing this stronghold; but it will undoubtedly take some time yet."[11] He was both correct and incorrect. Grant would order another assault before he relegated his forces to a siege.

Morale continued to drop for the Midwestern soldiers in the two days after the assault as they gathered their wounded and Confederates intermittently fired on the Union lines with both rifles and cannons. Davis continued in his notes of "Wednesday, May 20—Our men were busy till one o'clock last night, gathering in the wounded. . . . We occupy the same position today that we did yesterday. I saw several men killed to-day who stood close by me. They were picked off by the rebel sharpshooters."[12] This first taste of protracted warfare during the Vicksburg Campaign foreshadowed the future siege.

Additionally, the reality of the assaults began to trickle to the public as published casualty lists. Customarily, officers were reported first. Later as the casualties were tallied, the names of the enlisted men would be revealed. "From a Captain in the 81st Illinois regiment we learn that Col. A. [James] J. Dollins of that regiment lost his life. In one of the attacks made by order of Grant upon the rebel works. His regiment also suffered some loss. The 19th United States regulars went into battle with 200 men, and came out with only 80 men."[13]

Though spirits dipped after the May 19 assault, newspapers from most Midwestern states differed on their coverage of the May 22 assault. Newspapers from Ohio generally gave a positive spin on the day's events. The *Highland Weekly News* of Hillsborough, Ohio, published reports from a Union soldier who recorded his thoughts throughout the campaign from the rear of the army. The soldier's musings are positive; focusing on the small victories while explaining why the army did not capture the city on the hill that day. "To-day a general charge upon the enemy's works was ordered, and made, though I can not yet learn that at any point the works were completely carried.

The singularly rough nature of the ground makes it almost impossible to tell what we have to encounter before us, and rapidly fatigues the men. But we advance in this way steadily."[14] They also focused on the decline of Confederate resources: "The guns of the rebels reply to our shelling but seldom. They are evidently husbanding their ammunition, for they can get no further supply. I think they are short of artillery too. Their redoubts are constructed for field guns, and within the last three weeks Grant has captured about seventy of these."[15]

Further reassuring the public that the Confederates could not withstand the Union forces much longer, Ohio newspapers continued the narrative that the "rebels powerless to reply, as our skirmishers were close to the works, unerringly picking off the rebel gunners. . . . The rebels inside the fort couldn't show themselves above the parapets, without meeting death from our sharp-shooters."[16] Reinforcing these claims, the newspapers emphasized the control Union forces possessed over the city and its people. Reports of May 22 stated, "To-day they tried to cut their way out, but were driven back. The city is at our mercy."[17] They further claimed the inevitability of the situation. With Vicksburg surrounded, "[a]ll possibility of escape is cut off. Every living man, woman and child must fall into our hands."[18] Despite all the positive accounts, Ohio newspapers could not hide the casualty reports but managed to spin the news as favorably as they could. "From Vicksburg we have reports up to the 25th (Monday of this week.) At that time all was progressing as well as could be expected. Our forces suffered a heavy repulse on the 22d, but were not all discouraged. The loss on that day was about one thousand."[19] It is unclear exactly what the author meant by loss, but the total Union casualty figures for the second assault was three times that number with 502 men killed, 2,550 wounded, and 147 missing.[20]

Newspapers in other Midwestern states were not as optimistic as those in Ohio. Despite the negative reports, they were clearly more accurate. The *Chicago Tribune* bluntly stated, "No earthwork was carried," and Union forces "were compelled to fall back with a fearful list of killed and wounded."[21] Once the newspaper was able to get accurate Union casualty figures it published them, while comparing them to unknown Confederate losses: "A correct estimate of our loss on the 22d will place the figures at 2,500 killed and wounded. It is impossible to get an accurate statement so soon after the engagement. . . . The rebel loss was trifling, how much I can not say, but probably less than one-fourth of ours."[22] The newspapers even included gory details, particularly the casualties of their hometown men. The *Daily Evansville Journal* in Indiana reported, "Lieutenant Colonel [William F. Barter] Barton [sic], of the 24th Indiana, had his right hand shattered while grasping the colors of his regiment and endeavoring to rally his men in the heat of battle. The 11th and 12th Indiana lost about 250 men each. Captain [Felix G. Welman] Halman [*sic*], of the 24th, is killed."[23] Similarly, Colonel Edward Foster Hoge of the 113th Illinois reported to the *Chicago Tribune*, "The regiment is very badly cut up. The national colors were actually shot to pieces, flag staff and all. The regimental colors are safe, what there is of them. Both Color Sergeants were shot. . . . You can form no idea of what a terrible place Vicksburg is to take."[24]

Some papers embellished the facts to make the fighting sound bloodier than it really was. The *Joliet Signal* in Illinois added another assault on May 23 despite publishing the paper well after May 22. Their descriptions gave the Rebels greater credit for caring for the dead. "The rebel loss on Friday's (May 22) and Saturday's (May 23) battles was quite small and does not exceed 500 in all, while the Federal loss was several thousand. The stench was so great that a cessation of hostilities took place, and, by permission of General Grant, 5,000 rebel soldiers assisted in burying the Federal dead."[25] Though newspapers in states other than Ohio printed more negative stories, they recognized the shift in strategy but still reported, "Our Army Suffers Awfully," and "The fighting grows more desperate each day."[26]

Days after the two assaults, newspaper accounts changed slowly. Generally speaking, earlier reactions were guarded toward the outcome, the possibility of continued bloodshed through future assaults, and concern about an unknown threat. The *Urbana Union* reported six days after the last assault that the Union army "overstated the extent of the enemy's loss, and underrated our own. If the enemy have retired in force, we may expect a diversion of the war into Tennessee, with a desperate purpose of reaching Ohio."[27] A few days later, the *Ashtabula Weekly Telegraph* stated that things are beginning to look up, since "the patience and endurance shown by our army and navy for so many months is about being rewarded."[28] By the end of May, writers "felt buoyant and full of confidence as to the final result" of the assaults.[29] In early June, the fears of a Confederate attack by Joseph E. Johnston's "Army of Relief" on Grant's rear waned and confidence was restored when it became evident that the Union commander planned to lay siege to the city instead of risking more Midwesterners' lives. "Gen. Grant holds Vicksburg in the hollow of his hand. He can take it any day by assault, but prefers to take it by siege, to save the effusion of blood."[30] Despite the losses, "[t]he North-west is determined, in the language of Gen. [John A.] Logan to hew their way to the Gulf with the sword."[31]

With the monotony of the siege, Midwestern newspapers began focusing their attention on who was leading the Army of the Tennessee: General Ulysses S. Grant. Since Grant was born on the Ohio-Kentucky border at

Point Pleasant, Ohio, Midwestern writers favored him as their local son and took every opportunity to promote him. The *Ottawa Free Trader* of Illinois described him as "a modest, unassuming man, and a man of business, and very popular with the troops."[32] A writer from Lancaster, Ohio, went farther, commenting on Grant's victories, "If signal success and splendid achievements are indications of generalship, Gen. Grant must be ranked among the very first generals of the war. . . . Gen'l Grant has gone on steadily and even quietly accomplishing great results."[33] The *Cleveland Morning Leader* compared him to the most noted Union commander in the eastern theater, George B. McClellan. Grant was perceived as more aggressive and that "[h]e has followed up his victories as has not been done during the war, and in a way to put it the deepest blush of shame the dallying operations of McClellan in the Peninsula [Campaign]." Midwestern writers further list his accomplishments in the Vicksburg Campaign and conclude, "The bare recital makes one's blood boil with exultant rejoicing; the details will be written in history and sung in song. Grant's star is in the zenith."[34]

Even after the assaults were over and Grant began to besiege Vicksburg, writers used the lull in active fighting to provide perspective and maintain confidence in Grant and his Vicksburg Campaign. In Ohio they went so far as to compare Grant's achievement to that of Napoleon, "Victory! Victory!!— Victory has shone upon our banners in Grant's glorious campaign in the rear of Vicksburg. In a series of bloody engagements our soldiers have immortalized themselves. The record of the last fortnight's operations reminds us of Napoleon's first campaign in Italy. . . . It is clear that the rebels have been out generaled and out fought."[35] Writers realized the need to maintain the morale of the local populace. Granted, they wanted to keep their readers engaged and their subscriptions filled, but the small-town newspapers interacted with the people and kept their spirits up through praise of Grant and reassuring the public that their soldiers were going to succeed. "Will Grant take Vicksburg? Decidedly yes. The dangers of his superb, romantic campaign are past. While marching from Grand Gulf to Big Black, by the way of Jackson and Bolton, his progress was brilliant but perilous. A single mistake or disaster might have overwhelmed his army with remediless ruin. But the mistake was not made, the disaster did not come."[36]

As time progressed and official reports and news of casualties reached home, reporters were not as kind to the Union army or Grant and wrote negative comments about both. Influenced by the significant casualty rates, they did not question whether Grant would succeed but inquired about his decisions. In Joliet, Illinois, an article began by praising Grant's actions during the assaults, since he "was on the field, and his reckless exposure of himself caused unbounded enthusiasm among the privates." Despite this positive note, the article expressed "fearful apprehensions that the task before them [Union soldiers] was greater than they could accomplish. We hope for the best, but we fear that like McClellan before Richmond, Gen. Grant has not been properly sustained by the authorities at Washington."[37] Farther from Grant's home state, a Kansas reporter was blunt in his evaluation of the general. Blame was pointed not at Washington but at the man himself. Criticizing the bloody assaults of May 22, the newspaperman wrote, "There seems to have been some bad management. Our troops were not supported, and were cut off in insolated bands. Whether this was the result of bad generalship or of the rugged, uneven and contrary nature of the g[r]ound is not definitely known, but a good general should know the ground before he sends his men into inaccessible places to be sacrificed."[38]

Despite the immensity of the situation, the newspapers provided some levity, playing on rumors of Grant's insobriety and his spartan lifestyle. Well-documented rumors of drunkenness followed Grant throughout his military career, and the time just after the assaults was no exception. Instead of attacking Grant's insobriety, a writer in Cleveland used it to lampoon the South's opinions of the commanding general. "Perhaps Grant is, as his enemies love to tell of him, mad! Grant, an inebriate! his army a rabble, an armed mob! How glorious is madness! O, wine! thou art the precursor of victory! thy sparkle is but the gleam of glory."[39] The most common joke circulating the Midwestern newspapers was the example Grant set; he "disencumbered himself of everything, setting an example to his officers and men. He took neither a horse nor a servant, overcoat nor blanket, nor tent, nor camp-chest— not even a clean shirt. His only baggage consisted of a tooth-brush. . . . On the battle-field he was omnipresent, riding everywhere"[40] The *Daily Evansville Journal* responded to these humorous rumors by inquiring, "How in the mischief could he ride everywhere without a horse? We do not doubt that he took a horse with him, as well as several chews of tobacco."[41] Not wanting a good joke go to waste, the satire did not end there. Over a week later the same editor posted the following:

A paragraph is going the rounds stating that General Grant (the hero of Vicksburg) never carried any baggage for his own benefit, upon a march, excepting a tooth brush. The subject being under discussion at a tea table at Rochester, says the [Louisville] Democrat, a doubt was expressed as to the reliability of the assertion. A gentleman suggested that the General evidently intended to scour the face of the country. A lady rejoined that he meant to fly into the teeth of the enemy; but the climactric observation of the evening was to the effect that he only wanted a little brush with the rebels. Certainly in the cleaning out brush at Vicksburg Grant has made free use of his "powder."[42]

Grant's success on the battlefield brought not only humorous musings but also economic opportunities for Midwesterners. From the moment Grant sought to capture Vicksburg, the Midwest helped supply the army. While campaigning in Mississippi, the Army of the Tennessee supplemented their supplies from Confederate warehouses and locals they encountered. When Grant initiated the siege, there was a significant increase in demand for food and supplies. With the ranks of his army growing and the need for more equipment to effectively siege Vicksburg, the Midwest became the primary source for these logistical needs. Word quickly spread that Grant needed these supplies. "STEAMBOAT men, at St. Louis, say that the expenses of the Vicksburg expedition, for the single item of chartering steamers, are $40,000 a day!"[43]

With the Mississippi River closed to Midwestern commerce from the start of the Civil War, it was more difficult to ship heartland goods to market. Despite the construction of rail lines before the war, the Mississippi had been a major artery for trade, with goods floated down the river to New Orleans and then shipped by boat to New York or other trade centers. News of Grant's imminent victory started a movement to recapture this trading avenue and the profits lost since 1861. And Midwesterners saw economic opportunities in a city and region isolated by war.

> They seem to be calculating pretty confidently, up West, on Grant's success at Vicksburg. The Illinois Central Railroad has arrangements made for a daily line of steamboats from Cairo to New Orleans. The capture of Vicksburg will open an immense business on the Mississippi. Louisiana is destitute of cattle, mules, hay, oats and western products, which will be poured into New Orleans the moment Grant draws in his cordon about Vicksburg and knocks down the last rebel stronghold on the mighty river.[44]

Overall, the Vicksburg Campaign improved business for the Midwest. With the prospect of victory and reopening of the Mississippi, prices of staple goods went down. The *Emporia News* of Kansas reported, "Business has been very good in town, during the past week. The news from Vicksburg has had the effect of bringing down calico, coffee, etc. per yard, and coffee 40 cts. per lb."[45] Some businessmen, such as the owner of Helmick's Tin and Stove Store in Urbana, Ohio, even used the campaign to advertise wares. "Do you want to know how Grant came to make his plans for the capture of Vicksburg which has resulted so victoriously to our arms? If you will call in at Helmick's Tin and Stove Store, and take a good look at the many articles to be found there—articles of worth and convenience—you will discover that his prices are such as will suit the most economical buyer."[46] Economically, Vicksburg represented not just a strategy to winning the war but also an opportunity to return some semblance of normalcy to their lives.

Political reactions to the assaults are what one would expect, especially with the newspapers openly affiliated with political parties. Democratic papers derided Grant, a Republican, for the assaults, particularly the loss of life. "We know, though, for a certainty, that Gen. Grant has several times thrown great masses of troops upon the works, that terrible slaughter has ensued, and that our troops have been obliged to fall back under the murderous fire of the rebel guns. . . . Again and again they scaled these formidable barriers but again they recoiled from the bursting hail of hundreds of cannon streaming full in their exposed ranks."[47] The *McArthur Democrat* went so far as to imply that Grant was "one of the most reckless generals, hence we look for awful slaughter in his Army, move where it will." They blamed Grant for the deaths of Union men since there was "a want of co-operation between subordinate and superior officers and commands. Storming parties went gallantly forward, but were left to perish for want of support. Regiments and brigades advanced nobly, but only to be disappointed in their expectations of receiving success and help." The newspaper even stated that Grant's assault on May 22 led to the deaths of "a large number of field and company officers, from the fact that the rebels at Vicksburg had a chance to 'pick their men,' . . . Under cover of a breastwork there was nothing to hinder the rebels from selecting the leaders of our infantry columns as they marched up in face of their deadly fire." And it would not be a politically affiliated newspaper unless it promoted its favored party member by stating that Grant "has not the skill to save his men as McClellan did."[48]

Most interesting is the *Daily Ohio Statesman*'s reaction to an article published in the local rival Republican newspaper, the *Ohio State Journal*. The *Journal*'s article was titled "Abolitionist Victory," which as with any political response had a "spin" for the newspaper's own purposes. The *Statesman* responded to the article,

Prematurely called Vicksburg an "Abolitionist Victory!" What will our brave and gallant soldiers say, when they read this announcement? The noble men who went into this war to fight for the Union as it was, and the Constitution as it is, will learn with regret and astonishment, that the central organ of the Republican party of Ohio claims a noble achievement of their heroism and valor as an "Abolitionist Victory." The wives, the fathers, the mothers, the brothers, the sisters, and the other loved friends of the immortal dead, will weep again, and weep bitterer tears, when they read the Journal's announcement that the victory is only for the "Abolitionists."

Even in victory, political factions found ways to exploit each other.[49]

Midwestern political drama corresponded with the assaults as well. Clement Vallandigham, the noted leader of the Ohio Democratic Party, a Copperhead, and an officer in the Knights of the Golden Circle, gave a major speech on May 1, 1863, protesting the Abraham Lincoln administration. Three days later Union soldiers arrested Vallandigham for violating General Orders Number 38, which declared that "all persons found within our lines who commit acts for the benefit of the enemies of our country will be tried as spies or traitors, and, if convicted, will suffer death." News of his arrest and trial on May 19, the same day as the first assault, received notable attention in Midwestern newspapers.[50]

Some, such as the *Holmes County Farmer* in Millersburg, Ohio, defended Vallandigham. "The idea that the great peace agitator, who had been so bold, fearless, and out-spoken, in the cause of his country, against official usurpations, Government plunderers, Abolition disunionists and clerical hypocrits, should abstain from the expression of any offensive sentiment, must have made the caged lion look like a meek kitten, in the eyes of those around him, who expected to hear him roar and shake his mane, under the influence of uncontrollable passion, hatred and revenge."[51] The clear sentiment across the Midwest was in opposition of the controversial leader. "The arrest of Vallandigham has done one useful thing, it has stripped the mask off the Copperheads . . . has turned their position and exposed their concealed purpose to public view."[52] Vallandigham's critics rejoiced when a Cincinnati judge convicted him of sedition and sentenced him to be held in prison until the end of the war at Fort Warren in Boston, Massachusetts. Ten days later his sentencing was overturned. Instead of serving his sentence in a northern prison, he was excommunicated and ordered to cross Union lines to the South. Some were upset about his release because "instead of being hung, as he [Vallandigham] deserved, [he] has been sent South to his friends. This has stirred up the whole nest, and they are buzzing about as spitefully as so many wasps."[53]

Soldiers fighting at Vicksburg who tired of the political squabbling back home responded strongly to news of Vallandigham's trial and release. Captain J. H. Kimball of the 96th Ohio Volunteer Infantry expressed dismay to his hometown newspaper, the *Delaware Gazette* of Ohio. He believed people like Vallandigham and events such as the trial only emboldened the Confederacy. "One cannot talk with a rebel five minutes without his asserting that nearly one half the people in the loyal States are opposed to the Administration and the further prosecution of the war, and are in favor of peace and compromise on any terms which the South may condescend to dictate." Kimball places the political fighting into perspective of the larger war,

> Soldiers who for months have been exiled from home, friends and the comforts of life, who have endured the perils, hardships and exposures of a campaign in the malarious Southern swamps, and have met the rebels face to face in deadly combat, have forgotten petty, party politics, and no longer care for this or that man or party, on account of old political associations. We care not what a man has been; we measure him by what he is, and have but one standard, the old Jackson doctrine, "The Union—it must and shall be preserved."

He concludes his letter with a simple solution: "Show a united front at home, as we do in the army, and my word for it, the war will soon end."[54] Though the men on the front lines followed the political activities of their home states, their focus was to do what it took to win the war so they simply could return home.

Politics divided the Midwesterners, but the social responsibility they felt toward the soldiers united them. News of the assaults on the Confederate lines inspired doctors to leave their practices and travel down the Mississippi to treat wounded soldiers. Ohio was one of the first to respond: "Dr. I. W. Goddard of this place left for Vicksburg last week, by direction of the Governor [David Todd] and Surgeon General [Joseph Barnes]. Drs. Pierce and Wells of Texas in this county also went. The State has already sent down several boat loads of surgeons, nurses and supplies; and the authorities seem to be doing their duty in preparing for the relief of the Ohio wounded in Grant's army."[55] Indiana also sent "Dr's. E. Read and G. W. Clipplinger, of Terre Haute, who are on their way to Vicksburg in response to the call of Gov. [Oliver P.] Morton."[56] William Hannaman, president of the Indiana State Sanitarium Commission, also led a group of doctors to Vicksburg so that "hundreds of Indiana's brave sons" would have "their sufferings relieved through his instrumentality. They and their children's children will bless him."[57] The doctors took with them not only their skills but "a large quantity of Sanitary stores."[58]

Though farmers and merchants did not have the required skills of surgeons and doctors, they could still contribute to the health and morale of the fighting men. Shipping vegetables to nourish the soldiers was a significant priority for the citizens of Ohio. "We have now on board a large quantity of potatoes and other vegetables. I shall make every effort to get them below Vicksburg, running the blockade grows of course more and more hazardous with each successive attempt, as the vigilance of the enemy keeps pace with our own temerity." Shipments of vegetables were not new during the conflict but with an army entrenched for a siege it was vital to keeping up their spirits. "I have received grateful and abundant testimony to the value of such disbursements from officers and surgeons in great numbers."[59] F. W. Bingham, an Ohio state agent, concurred in a letter to Mrs. B. Rouse of the President Soldiers' Society: "The improved condition on the health of the troops, is said to be attributable in a small degree to the liberal issue of vegetables to the army by the Government and United States Sanitary Commission. There is still an urgent demand upon the country for continued effort in your blessed work." Additionally, Bingham praised the society for "the valuable collection of books and pamphlets prepared by Mrs. Dr. Aikin[.] I take occasion to say that reading matter is highly prized by the soldiers."[60] Though only small comforts, the additional food and reading material broke up the monotony of army life when there was no active fighting.

The Sanitation Commission, a private organization, supported the war effort, particularly "promoting the health, comfort and efficiency of the vast armies called into the field to subdue the rebellion."[61] The commission used the assaults to renew their impassioned call to support "[t]hose who still live, after a campaign of unexampled endurance and unsurpassed bravery, now stand up with firm, bare breasts in front of the deadly cannon and rifle pits at Vicksburg—exhausted by fatigue and short rations." They explained that the soldiers' actions

> sustain the government and give value to our property; enable us to carry on our business and pleasure; to worship in our churches; to preserve our grain warehouses, fruitful fields, sleek stock and well-filled barns; to enable us to sit under our own vine and fig tree, and gather our wives and children around us at home, while they fight, die, and are maimed yonder—under a broiling sun by day, insects and malaria by night—unsheltered by a tent.

In response to their action, should Midwesterners "refuse to pour out supplies and money to the point of self-denial, for, God only knows, how many thousand wounded now, and more to follow?"[62] The social support for the men wounded in the assaults, but who continued to besiege the Confederates, was swift and significant.

Regional studies are still relatively overlooked by historians and usually deemed too provincial to be taken seriously. But from the study of the Midwesterners' reactions to the assaults at Vicksburg, many details are revealed. The people of the region, like others elsewhere, followed more closely the campaigning that directly impacted their lives and those of their loved ones in the army. Through the fog of war details, newspaper reports can be incorrect and skewed, while others enlighten us on the trials soldiers faced. Morale back home was just as important as that in camp. After the last assault and preparation by Grant's army for a siege, active editing replaced all the accounts of fighting. Positive descriptions of Grant helped maintain morale and sometimes levity in a time of conflict. Most important, the assaults revealed the economic, political, and social impact that the imminent capture of Vicksburg would bring. Midwesterners, despite their political leanings, saw Vicksburg as one step closer to victory and a return to their lives before the war.

Notes

1. MapQuest.com, a website that provides distances between different geographical points, shows the distance between Vicksburg, Mississippi, and the southern tip of Missouri, the closest Midwestern state border, is approximately three hundred miles. Vicksburg is about 430 miles from Springfield, Missouri, the closest significant city, and around 435 miles from St. Louis, Missouri, the closest major city. Around the times of the assaults Lee's Army of Northern Virginia was near Chancellorsville, Virginia. Lee's army was approximately three hundred miles from the Ohio border and 415 miles from Columbus, Ohio, the closest major Midwestern city. www.mapquest.com.

2. U.S. War Department, *The War of the Rebellion: A Compilation of the Official Records of the Union and Confederate Armies*, 128 vols. (Washington, DC, 1880–1901), ser. 1, vol. 24, pt. 2: 148–58. Hereinafter cited as *OR*. All references are to series 1 unless otherwise indicated.

3. *OR*, vol. 27, pt. 1: 155–68.

4. *Grand Haven (KS) News*, May 27, 1863.

5. *Cleveland Morning Leader*, May 25, 1863.

6. Steven E. Woodworth and Charles D. Grear, eds., *The Vicksburg Campaign: March 29–May 18* (Carbondale: University of Southern Illinois University, 2013); Michael B. Ballard, *Vicksburg: The Campaign That Opened the Mississippi* (Chapel Hill: University of North Carolina University Press, 2004), 327–29.

7. *Urbana (OH) Union*, May 27, 1863.

8. *Cadiz (OH) Democratic Sentinel*, May 27, 1863.

9. Margie Riddle Bearss, "The Capture of Haynes Bluff by the 4th Iowa Cavalry," *Annals of Iowa* 40, no. 5 (Summer 1970): 338.

10. *Daily Ohio Statesman* (Columbus), June 5, 1863.

11. Ibid., June 2, 1863.

12. Ibid., June 5, 1863.

13. *Chicago Tribune,* May 30, 1863.

14. *Highland Weekly News* (Hillsborough, OH), June 4, 1863.

15. *Cleveland Morning Leader,* June 2, 1863; *Highland Weekly News,* June 4, 1863.

16. *Cleveland Morning Leader,* June 2, 1863; *Highland Weekly News,* June 4, 1863.

17. *Cleveland Morning Leader,* May 30, 1863.

18. *Daily Ohio Statesman,* May 28, 1863.

19. *Cleveland Morning Leader,* May 30, 1863.

20. Edwin C. Bearss, *The Vicksburg Campaign,* vol. 3, *Unvexed to the Sea* (Dayton, OH: Morningside Press, 1986), 869.

21. *Chicago Tribune,* May 30, 1863.

22. Ibid., June 2, 1863.

23. *Daily Evansville (IN) Journal,* May 30, 1863.

24. *Chicago Tribune,* May 30, 1863.

25. *Joliet (IL) Signal,* June 9, 1863; Ballard, *Vicksburg,* 348–50; Bearss, *Vicksburg Campaign,* 3: 860–61.

26. *Daily Evansville Journal,* June 2, 1863; *Nebraska Advertiser* (Brownville, Nebraska Territory), June 4, 1863.

27. *Urbana Union,* May 27, 1863.

28. *Ashtabula (OH) Weekly Telegraph,* May 30, 1863.

29. *Chicago Tribune,* May 31, 1863.

30. Ibid., June 2, 1863; *Ottawa (IL) Free Trader,* June 6, 1863.

31. *Daily Evansville Journal,* June 4, 1863.

32. Brooks D. Simpson, *Ulysses S. Grant: Triumph over Adversity, 1822–1865* (New York: Houghton Mifflin, 2000), 2–3; *Ottawa Free Trader,* June 6, 1863.

33. *Weekly Lancaster (OH) Gazette,* May 28, 1863.

34. *Cleveland Morning Leader,* May 26, 1863.

35. *Delaware (OH) Gazette,* May 29, 1863.

36. *Daily Ohio Statesman,* May 31, 1863.

37. *Joliet Signal,* June 2, 1863.

38. *Independent* (Oskaloosa, KS), June 6, 1863.

39. *Cleveland Morning Leader,* May 30, 1863.

40. *Daily Evansville Journal,* May 27, 1863; *East Saginaw (MI) Courier,* June 2, 1863; *White Cloud Kansas Chief,* June 4, 1863.

41. *Daily Evansville Journal,* May 27, 1863.

42. Ibid., June 5, 1863; *Tiffin (OH) Weekly Tribune,* June 5, 1863.

43. *Grand Haven (KS) News,* May 27, 1863.

44. *Cleveland Morning Leader,* May 19, 1863.

45. *Emporia (KS) News,* May 30, 1863. Calico is a semicoarse cotton cloth that was commonly used to make clothes.

46. *Urbana Union,* May 27, 1863.

47. *Holmes County Farmer* (Millersburg, OH), June 4, 1863.

48. *McArthur (OH) Democrat,* June 4, 1863; *Chicago Tribune,* June 2, 1863.

49. *Ohio State Journal,* May 26, 1863; *Daily Ohio Statesman,* May26, 1863.

50. Frank Abial Flower, *Edwin McMasters Stanton: The Autocrat of Rebellion, Emancipation, and Reconstruction* (New York: Saalfield Publishing Company, 1905), 250, 252; "General Orders, No. 38 (DOO)," *Ohio Civil War Central,* retrieved July 26, 2017, http://www.ohiocivilwarcentral.com/entry.php?rec=104.

51. *Holmes County Farmer*, June 4, 1863.

52. *Chicago Tribune*, May 30, 1863.

53. Flower, *Edwin McMasters Stanton*, 252; *Chicago Tribune*, May 30, 1863.

54. *Delaware (OH) Gazette*, May 29, 1863.

55. *Urbana Union*, June 3, 1863.

56. *Daily Evansville Journal*, May 26, 1863.

57. Ibid., May 27, 1863.

58. Ibid., May 30, 1863.

59. *Cleveland Morning Leader*, May 30, 1863; November, 21, 1863.

60. Ibid., May 30, 1863.

61. Charles Stillé, *History of the United States Sanitary Commission, being the general report of its work during the War of the Rebellion* (Philadelphia: J. B. Lippincott and Company, 1866), 19.

62. *Marshall County Republican* (Plymouth, IN), June 4, 1863.

CONTRIBUTORS
INDEX

CONTRIBUTORS

Brandon Franke serves as dean for the social sciences at Blinn College, teaching there previously for eighteen years. His other published works include "Waul's Texas Legion: Towards Vicksburg" and "A Century along the Brazos: The Futile Attempts to Tame a Texas River."

Charles D. Grear teaches at Central Texas College. He has written extensively on the involvement of Texas in the Civil War, including *Why Texans Fought in the Civil War* (2010), and has edited several books, among them *The Tennessee Campaign* (with Steven E. Woodworth, 2016) and *The Fate of Texas* (2008).

J. Parker Hills retired from the Mississippi Army National Guard with the rank of brigadier general. He is a graduate of the U.S. Army War College and holds a master's degree from Sul Ross State University. In addition to his years of military service and leadership training, he has presided over several historic Civil War battlefield commissions and has authored numerous articles and books on American history and the Civil War. His books include *A Study in Warfighting: Nathan Bedford Forrest and the Battle of Brice's Crossroads* (1995); *The Vicksburg Campaign Driving Tour Guide* (coauthored with the late Warren Grabau, 2008); *Receding Tide: Vicksburg and Gettysburg, the Campaigns That Changed the Civil War* (coauthored with Edwin C. Bearss, 2010); and *Art of Commemoration: Vicksburg National Military Park* (2012).

Steven E. Woodworth teaches at Texas Christian University and has authored, coauthored, or edited thirty-one books on the Civil War era, among them *Nothing but Victory: The Army of the Tennessee, 1861–1865* (2006) and *Jefferson Davis and His Generals: The Failure of Confederate Command in the West* (1990).

INDEX

Alabama troops: 20th Infantry, 46, 63, 79, 81–82, 89; 30th Infantry, 45, 79, 81–83; 42nd Infantry, 44; 46th Infantry, 63, 89
Army of Mississippi, 4
Army of Northern Virginia, 109
Army of Relief, 1, 3, 5, 101
Army of Tennessee, 74, 78, 86
Army of the Mississippi, 1–2, 86
Army of the Tennessee, 1–4, 7, 33, 64, 68–69, 94, 101, 104
Army of West Tennessee, 73
Ashtabula Weekly Telegraph (Ohio), 101
Atherton, J. B., 69–70
Atlanta Campaign, 42

Badeau, Adam, 12, 20
Baldwin, William E., 78
Baldwin's Ferry Road, 7, 9, 16–17, 20, 25, 31, 43–44, 57, 74
Barnes, Joseph, 107
Barter, William F., 100
Battery Maloney, 42–43, 45–46, 50
Battery McPherson, 53
Benton, William P., 43–44, 86
Big Black River Bridge, 1, 9, 12, 17, 32, 57, 59–60, 75–76, 86, 98, 102
Bingham, F. W., 108
Blair, Frank, 8–9, 11–14, 20, 34–36
Blanchard, Ira, 37
Bolton, Mississippi, 102
Bonaparte, Napoléon, 42, 102
Boomer, George B., 16, 32–33, 38–41, 50, 67–68, 81, 84, 89
Boston, Massachusetts, 106
Bowen, John S., 4, 19–20, 75
Bowers, Theodore S., 50
Bradley, L. D., 82–85
Bragg, Braxton, 49
Brenham, Texas, 73
Brewer, George, 89
Bridgeport Road, 7, 9–10, 22
Bruinsburg, Mississippi, 73, 98
Burbridge, Stephen G., 17, 43–44, 50

Cadwallader, Sylvanus, 11
Cairo, Illinois, 104

Camp Fisk, 23
Camp Waul, 73
Campbell, John Quincy Adams, 39–40, 76–78, 81, 84, 86, 89
Canton, Mississippi, 74
Carman, Isaac H., 83
Carr, Eugene A., 9, 17, 43, 46–47, 50, 59–60, 68, 84–85
Chalmers, James Ronald, 87
Champion Hill, Battle of, 9, 12, 22, 41–42, 57, 61, 65, 75, 89
Chancellorsville, Battle of, 97, 109
Chicago Times, 11
Chicago Tribune, 100–101
Chickasaw Bayou, 10
Cincinnati, Ohio, 106
City of Tokio (steamship), 11, 27
Clausewitz, Carl von, 41
Cleveland, Ohio, 98, 103
Cleveland Morning Leader, 102
Clipplinger, G. W., 107
Cockrell, Francis M., 19–20, 35
Cold Harbor, Battle of, 51
Columbus, Ohio, 99, 109
Cook's Bayou, 9
Copperhead, 96, 106
Council-of-War, 1
Countryman Road, 7–8, 10, 21–22
Crocker, Marcellus M., 41
Culkin, Mississippi, 22

Daily Evansville Journal (Indiana), 100, 103
Daily Ohio Statesman (Columbus), 99, 105
Davis, Jefferson, 75
Davis, William M., 99
Delaware Gazette (Ohio), 107
Democratic Party, 105–6
Dollins, James J., 38, 99
Dr. Cook's plantation, 10, 24
Dunlap, Cornelius, 46, 63
Dupeire's battalion, 88
Durden Creek, 16, 18, 25
Durden Ridge, 16–18, 25

Edgar, William, 73
Edward's Depot, 74
Edwards, Mississippi, 9

The Bridge Street
HISTORY CENTER
Granbury, Texas

The Bridge Street History Center is in Granbury, Hood County, Texas. The city and the county were named for Confederate Civil War generals Hiram B. Granbury and John Bell Hood. The mission of the Bridge Street History Center is to "collect, preserve and interpret the life stories of the people of Granbury and Hood County and to examine how they illuminate the history of America." To learn more, visit http://bshc-granbury.org/wp/.

CIVIL WAR CAMPAIGNS IN THE WEST

The area west of the Appalachian Mountains, known in Civil War parlance as "the West," has always stood in the shadow of the more famous events on the other side of the mountains, the eastern theater, where even today hundreds of thousands visit the storied Virginia battlefields. Nevertheless, a growing number of Civil War historians believe that the outcome of the war was actually decided in the region east of the Mississippi River and west of the watershed between the Atlantic and the Gulf of Mexico.

Modern historians began to rediscover the decisive western theater in the 1960s through the work of the late Thomas Lawrence Connelly, particularly his 1969 book *Army of the Heartland*, in which he analyzed the early years of the Confederacy's largest army in the West. Many able scholars have subsequently contributed to a growing historiography of the war in the West. Despite recent attention to the western theater, less is understood about the truly decisive campaigns of the war than is the case with the dramatic but ultimately indecisive clashes on the east coast.

Several years ago, three of Steven E. Woodworth's graduate students pointed out that the western theater possessed no series of detailed multi-author campaign studies comparable to the excellent and highly acclaimed series Gary W. Gallagher has edited on the campaigns of the eastern theater. Charles D. Grear, Jason M. Frawley, and David Slay joined together in suggesting that Woodworth ought to take the lead in filling the gap. The result is this series. Its goals are to shed more light on the western campaigns and to spark new scholarship on the western theater.

CIVIL WAR CAMPAIGNS IN THE WEST SERIES

The Shiloh Campaign

The Chickamauga Campaign

The Chattanooga Campaign

The Vicksburg Campaign, March 29–May 18, 1863

The Tennessee Campaign of 1864

The Vicksburg Assaults, May 19–22, 1863

The first five books were published under the series title "Civil War Campaigns in the Heartland."